THE ART OF WOODWORKING

HANDBOOK OF JOINERY

THE ART OF WOODWORKING

HANDBOOK OF JOINERY

TIME-LIFE BOOKS
ALEXANDRIA, VIRGINIA

ST. REMY PRESS
MONTREAL • NEW YORK

THE ART OF WOODWORKING was produced by
ST. REMY PRESS

PUBLISHER	Kenneth Winchester
PRESIDENT	Pierre Léveillé
Series Editor	Pierre Home-Douglas
Series Art Director	Francine Lemieux
Senior Editors	Marc Cassini (Text)
	Heather Mills (Research)
Art Directors	Normand Boudreault, Luc Germain,
	Solange Laberge
Designers	Jean-Guy Doiron, Michel Giguère,
	Hélène Dion
Research Editor	Jim McRae
Picture Editor	Christopher Jackson
Writers	Andrew Jones, Rob Lutes
Research Assistant	Bryan Quinn
Contributing Illustrators	Gilles Beauchemin, Rolland Bergera,
	Jean-Pierre Bourgeois, Michel Blais,
	Ronald Durepos, Robert Paquet,
	James Thérien
Administrator	Natalie Watanabe
Production Manager	Michelle Turbide
System Coordinator	Jean-Luc Roy
Photographer	Robert Chartier
Proofreader	Judith Yelon
Indexer	Christine M. Jacobs

Time-Life Books is a division of Time-Life Inc.,
a wholly owned subsidiary of
THE TIME INC. BOOK COMPANY

TIME-LIFE BOOKS

President	John D. Hall
Vice-President	Nancy K. Jones
Editor-in-Chief	Thomas H. Flaherty
Director of Editorial Resources	Elise D. Ritter-Clough
Marketing Director	Regina Hall
Editorial Director	Lee Hassig
Consulting Editor	John R. Sullivan
Production Manager	Marlene Zack

THE CONSULTANTS

Jon Arno is a consultant, cabinetmaker and freelance writer who lives in Troy, Michigan. He also conducts seminars on wood identification and early American furniture design.

Giles Miller-Mead taught advanced cabinet-making at Montreal technical schools for more than ten years. A native of New Zealand, he has worked as a restorer of antique furniture.

Joseph Truini is Senior Editor of *Home Mechanix* magazine. A former Shop and Tools Editor of *Popular Mechanics*, he has worked as a cabinetmaker, home improvement contractor and carpenter.

Handbook of Joinery
p. cm.—(The Art of Woodworking)
Includes index.
ISBN 0-8094-9941-X (trade)
ISBN 0-8094-9942-8 (lib)
1. Joinery
I. Time-Life Books. II. Series
TH5663.H36 1993
694'.6—dc20   93-24638
                                    CIP

For information about any Time-Life book,
please call 1-800-621-7026, or write:
Reader Information
Time-Life Customer Service
P.O. Box C-32068
Richmond, Virginia
23261-2068

CONTENTS

Mike Dunbar discusses

MAKING WINDSOR CHAIRS

I have been making Windsor chairs for 20 years and I am still as fascinated with them as when I began. This chair's durability is legendary—a fame that is well earned. There are many Windsor chairs that have survived 200 years or more of hard use but remain as solid as the day they were built. The secret is in the joints, which are highly engineered.

Like most common chairs, Windsors use socket construction—a round tenon that fits into a round hole. There is very little edge grain around the circumference of a hole to create a good glue joint. Because most of the circumference is end grain, a round tenon in a drilled hole is a very poor joint that soon comes apart. Its only virtue is that it can be produced quickly and easily. To make it work some additional strengthening is required.

The major joints in a Windsor are those that connect the turned legs to the seat. These are held together with a locking taper, similar to the device that holds—or locks—the drive center in a lathe's headstock. The leg tenon is made cone-like while the part is still in the lathe. The hole in the seat is then fitted to the tenon with a tapered reamer, a type of conical bit inserted in a brace, like the one I'm holding in the photograph. When assembled, the tenon and matching hole lock together, securing the joint. Should the joint ever loosen, the weight of a person sitting in the chair tightens it again, whereas in other types of chairs the act of sitting actually wears the joints.

A Windsor's legs are connected by a stretcher system. The chairmaker ensures that these joints remain permanently secure by assembling them under compression. The trick is to measure the distance between the legs while the chair is being assembled. The stretchers are then made slightly longer than the measured distance. Being a tad too long, they push the legs apart. For their part, the legs hold the joints in compression. As a result, they cannot come apart—even if the glue fails.

Mike Dunbar builds fine furniture at his workshop in Portsmouth, New Hampshire. The author of seven books and a contributing editor of American Woodworker *and* Early American Life *magazines, Dunbar also offers Windsor chairmaking seminars across North America.*

Lyle Kruger talks about

JIGS AND JOINTS

A s a young boy, the best toys that I possessed were—in order—Tinker Toys, Lincoln Logs, an Erector set, and American Flyer electric trains. These toys prepared me for an adulthood in which I am not afraid to tackle complex mechanical problems.

As most of my power tools are older models (my table saw is a 1940s Sears that I inherited from my wife's grandfather), I must get as much accuracy as I can from my various jigs and attachments. Over the years I have found that, with a bit of time and patience, you can adjust and fine-tune many older tools and make them perform almost as well as the day they left the factory. I get a certain satisfaction out of restoring these auction and garage sale bargains to usable items.

I take delight in applying one technology to another discipline. The home-made tenoning jig in the photo, for example, works much like the cross feed on a metal lathe. It slides back and forth on ways made of walnut and features a feed screw that indexes movement to ¹⁄₆₄ inch. With a little thought and extra care in the finish, these jigs can become heirloom-quality and be passed down through a family with pride. I would even suggest that you sign and date your better jigs.

I find that when I am in my shop trying to figure out a problem or a better way to build a jig, my creative juices get going and time seems to fly by. Before I know it, the evening is over—and I've missed the final baseball scores on the radio.

Recently I have experimented with a Southwestern-American-inspired joint that locks together without glue and yet is still very strong. This joint has a stepped corner and a special key that slides into a mortise and locks the joint. It can be made on the table saw with the help of a couple of shop-made jigs and on the drill press fitted with a mortising bit. The stepped corner is cut without changing the blade or fence setting on the table saw.

Lyle Kruger is a professional land surveyor from Effingham, Illinois, who enjoys building full-scale wooden replicas of antique survey instruments. He has published articles and shop tips on woodworking in various magazines.

Pat Warner on

JOINERY AND THE ROUTER

I am a designer-craftsman of contemporary furniture and cabinets. I use hardwood lumber for nearly everything I make. There are, however, occasions when I must use plywood or fiberboard, such as in drawer bottoms, door panels, or cabinet backs. While they are often essential, I don't find these materials as enjoyable to work as solid lumber, since the wood joinery methods I often use cannot be applied to them. Plywood is glued up in layers that lie in so many different planes that it cannot achieve the structure of solid wood. Solid lumber, on the other hand, consists of cells that are distinctly oriented—like a bundle of straws. This long-axis architecture, in my view, allows many joinery possibilities. No matter how complex the piece of furniture, there is always a means of joining the pieces together.

I find the electric router very handy for joinery because of its ability to accept a wide variety of jigs, fixtures, and accessories. Whether the tool is guided by a piloted cutter, an edge guide, a template collar or sub-base, or secured in a table, the router provides the kind of control that makes it ideally useful for joinery. No other single power tool can produce the same range of joints, including tongues, grooves, rabbets, tenons, mortises, dadoes, dovetails, laps, notches, fingers, and keys. Complementary template joinery—or joinery along curved lines—can only be done with a router. The tool can also be used to make the precision templates required for the process.

Because it is so useful a tool, I have collected 18 different routers. They can be coupled with any number of accessories, jigs, and cutters to expand their joint-making capabilities. Fortunately, this is usually quite simple and inexpensive. Most router jigs are easy to make and use.

Most of my portable routing is done with the assistance of an acrylic offset sub-base like the one attached to the router in the photo. It provides extra support on the base, making it indispensable for routing certain templates. Another jig that I find handy is my tenoning jig; in the photo it is upside down with the workpiece clamped in place against an adjustable fence. I like to use it with a plunge router, which can be adjusted to cut different depths more easily than a standard router. Both jigs have proved so useful that I have started manufacturing them for the commercial market.

Pat Warner makes contemporary furniture in Escondido, California, and works as a consultant for the router and tool bit industry. He is a contributing editor for Woodwork *magazine and teaches routing at Palomar Community College in San Marcos.*

JOINERY BASICS

Joinery, the foundation of woodworking, is a subtle blend of art and engineering. Whether the product is a simple tabletop or an ornate chest, its joinery will establish its worth: Strong joints will give it longevity, and their design and craftsmanship will enhance its beauty.

The need for jointmaking derives from the fact that woodworkers make demands on their material that nature never intended. Interlocking curves of fiber link a branch to the tree trunk, while a leg is attached to a table at an abrupt 90° intersection. Thus, although a properly glued joint is stronger than wood fiber, that bond alone is seldom able to withstand the forces exerted on tables, chairs, cabinets, and doors during normal use.

Most joints need some sort of mechanical aid—a reinforcement designed to meet the stresses head-on. From that need springs the craft of joinery.

The simplest supports are nails, screws, splines, biscuits, and dowels. These require simply cutting a hole and adding wood or metal to the intersection of the pieces. Often, this is enough to satisfy structural and esthetic needs.

Sometimes—most often when furniture is involved—greater strength and beauty are called for. The solution then is to cut the intersecting pieces so that the gluing area is increased or they form an interlocking bond.

The blind and through mortise-and-tenon joints shown below at right improve the strength of a right-angle joint and increase the long-grain glu-

ing area. The blind version also partially conceals the joint; the through version, in which the tenon passes through the mating workpiece, can be tightened by the addition of small wedges.

In addition to lending mechanical strength and gluing area to a connection, joinery must also allow for the movement of wood—its swelling and shrinkage as it absorbs and releases moisture. The best joinery relates all three needs.

The stresses on joints and some ways to relieve them are detailed on the facing page. Wood's moisture-absorbing characteristics are discussed on pages 14 and 15. Joint selection is discussed on pages 16 and 17. Pages 18 and 19 contain useful information about choosing and using glues and clamps.

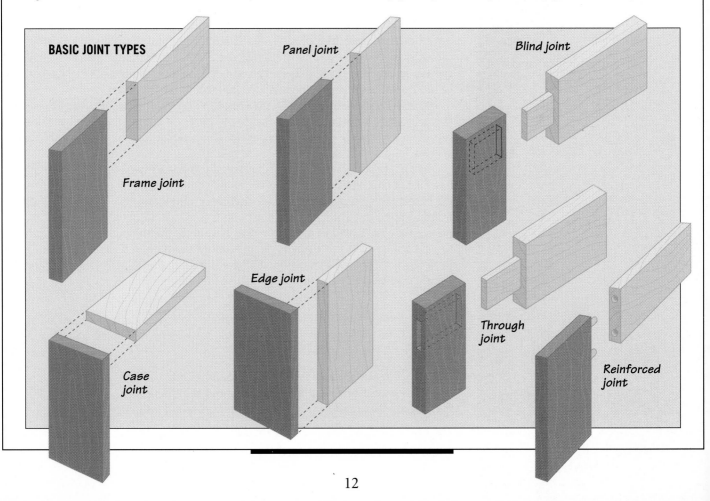

BASIC JOINT TYPES

Frame joint

Case joint

Panel joint

Edge joint

Blind joint

Through joint

Reinforced joint

TYPES OF STRESS

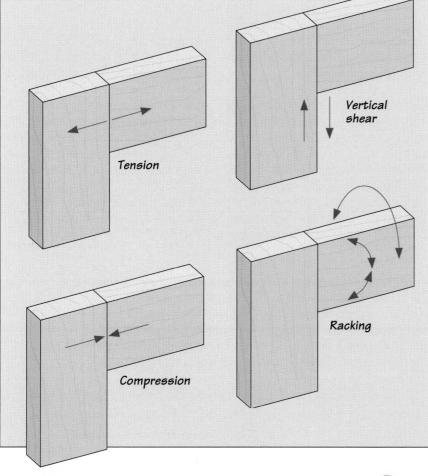

Tension

Vertical shear

Compression

Racking

Recognizing the stresses on joints

The illustration at left shows the four basic types of forces that affect joints: compression, tension, vertical shear, and racking. Compression forces a joint together, while tension pulls it apart. A typical example of tension is an overloaded shelf joined to a carcase with dado joints; the weight on the shelf will tend to pull the shelf out of the dadoes. Vertical shear occurs when the two halves of a joint slide against each other, common with butt joints. Racking, characterized by twisting and bending, is the toughest stress for a joint to endure.

IMPROVING A JOINT'S RESISTANCE TO STRESS

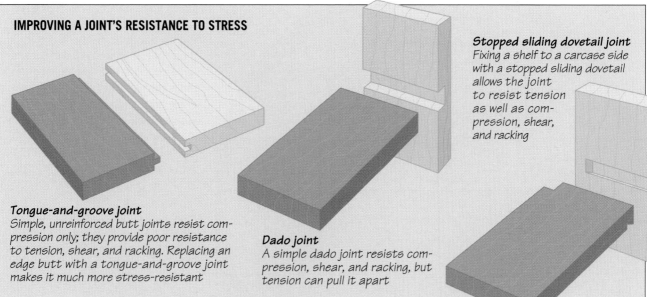

Stopped sliding dovetail joint
Fixing a shelf to a carcase side with a stopped sliding dovetail allows the joint to resist tension as well as compression, shear, and racking

Tongue-and-groove joint
Simple, unreinforced butt joints resist compression only; they provide poor resistance to tension, shear, and racking. Replacing an edge butt with a tongue-and-groove joint makes it much more stress-resistant

Dado joint
A simple dado joint resists compression, shear, and racking, but tension can pull it apart

WOOD MOVEMENT

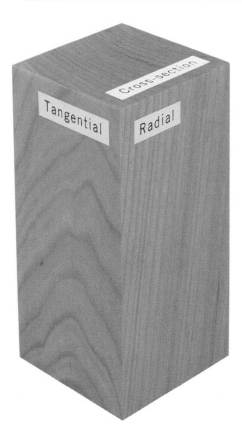

Scientists describe wood as a hygroscopic material—that is, it absorbs moisture. Long after a tree has been felled and its wood milled and made into furniture, the fibrous cells absorb and release moisture, mirroring the humidity of the surrounding air.

The consequences for the woodworker can be serious: Wood swells as it absorbs moisture and shrinks as it expels it, causing motion that accounts for most failed joints, wobbly chairs, sticking doors, and split picture frames.

Although wood movement is unavoidable, such consequences are not: An understanding of wood's characteristics will enable you to accommodate this swelling and contraction and produce joinery that is both durable and stable.

The wood of most species is characterized by growth rings, which are concentric bands perpendicular to the axis of the trunk. The manner in which the rings are exposed on a wood surface can help you anticipate how the piece will react to humidity changes. As the illustration below shows, there is more swelling and shrinkage along the growth rings than across them. The way lumber is cut from a log has a crucial effect on how much the wood will shrink and which dimension—length, width, or thickness—will be most affected.

Any piece of wood provides three views of the annual growth rings. The transverse section—or cross section—lies at right angles to the grain and is visible in the end grain of stock. The tangential and radial sections are at right angles to the transverse section. Being able to distinguish the different views of the rings on a workpiece can help you compensate for wood movement in your joinery.

GROWTH RINGS AND MOVEMENT

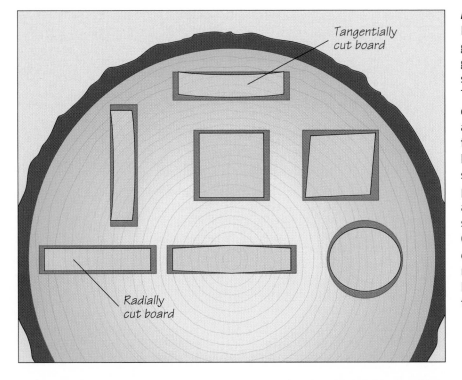

Anticipating wood movement

Lumber does not shrink uniformly. Tangential shrinkage—parallel to the annual growth rings—is almost twice the radial shrinkage, which occurs across the rings. This difference accounts for the warping of boards and panels as wood contracts and expands with fluctuations in moisture content. Radially cut boards, also known as quartersawn, are more dimensionally stable than tangentially cut, or plain-sawn boards because they shrink and swell less across their width. Plain-sawn boards tend to cup at the edges. Greater tangential than radial shrinkage can cause square boards to become diamond shaped and cylindrical ones to become oval, as shown by the pieces on the right-hand side of the illustration.

Logs are sawn in two basic ways, with many variations. The most common system, called plain-sawing, slices the log tangent to the growth rings. The other method, less commonly used, is called quartersawing or edge-grain sawing. It takes slices at right angles to the growth rings. Although the techniques used in each system are very different, each will produce some boards with characteristics of the other. For example, plain-sawing through the center of a log produces a piece of stock that looks much like a quarter-sawn board.

Quartersawn boards have their annual growth rings perpendicular to the face. This orientation of the growth rings accounts for the superior dimensional stability of quartersawn boards. Wood shrinks and expands roughly twice as much tangentially to the rings as its does radially. When quartersawn boards swell or shrink they do so mostly in thickness, which is minimal, whereas a plain-sawn board changes across its width. A table made from plain-sawn pine boards, for example, can change as much as 1 inch in width; a similar table made from quartersawn boards would only swell or shrink by one-quarter as much or less, depending on the species.

Although you may not be able to control the environment where your furniture will be used, you can make your joinery choices to compensate for wood movement. Orient the growth rings in the mating pieces of a joint so that they move together. For example, the rings of the two parts of a corner joint should be parallel to each other so that they shrink or swell in tandem. When the rings of the pieces meet at right angles, as in a mortise-and-tenon joint, make sure their tangential surfaces are aligned.

Workpieces that feature irregular grain require particular attention. A square chair leg with growth rings that run diagonally through it when viewed in cross section, for example, will eventually lose its square shape and become a diamond shape, pulling the chair frame out of square with it.

The annual growth rings in the plain-sawn oak board (top) *appear on the face as an elliptical landscape figure. Plain-sawn stock is sliced tangent to the rings. The growth rings in the quartersawn oak board* (bottom) *appear as lines perpendicular to the face.*

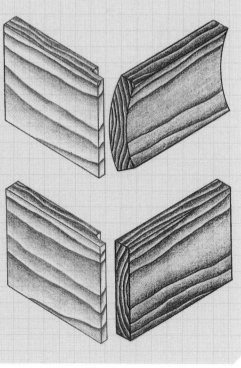

SHOP TIP

**The importance
of grain alignment**
A drawer glued up from plain-sawn boards illustrates how grain alignment can make or break a joint. By aligning the boards so that the annual growth rings curve inward (top), the joint may separate at the top and bottom when the front cups as it dries. If the boards are aligned so that the annual rings curve outward (bottom), drying of the wood will tend push the top and bottom toward the mating piece, keeping the joint together.

FORM AND FUNCTION

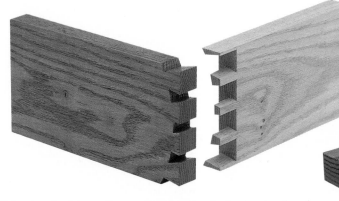

Selecting the joinery for a project involves both structural and esthetic considerations. The curved through dovetail (above) blends strength and attractiveness for drawers that will be the highlight of a piece. The utilitarian dado joint (right) is a good choice to anchor the shelving in a modern cabinet.

I deally, joinery should achieve a balance between form and function. Each joint must complement the overall design of a piece while resisting the stresses to which it will be subjected.

The choice of a joint will often be dictated by its function and location. Carcase corners can be joined with a host of joinery methods, but a carcase that is more likely to be visible, such as a drawer, will benefit from a visually pleasing joint like a half-blind dovetail or box joint. For other project components, the options are more limited. A frame-and-panel door, for example, may call for either blind or haunched mortise-and-tenons, while a chair with round rungs should ideally be assembled with round mortise-and-tenons.

The wood you choose will also have a bearing on your options. The chart opposite lists the various joints shown in this book and rates their utility with

solid wood, plywood, and particleboard. A joint like the frame butt, for example, can be used with any material, but only if the connection is reinforced. (As a rule of thumb, any joint involving end grain must be reinforced in some way.) The dovetail, while it requires no reinforcement, is only appropriate with solid wood.

Once you have chosen your joinery, prepare your stock. Carefully joint and smooth all mating surfaces. The following chapters illustrate dozens of joints and provide detailed instructions for making them. If you are unsure about which joint to select for a given application, choose the simplest one, particularly if it will be hidden.

JOINERY TIPS

• Avoid working with freshly cut lumber, as it will shrink after the joint is assembled. Use wood that has dried to a moisture content approximating the level of the environment in which the finished piece will be used.

• When designing a piece of furniture that will bear a heavy load, use larger joints or joints with larger structural members, such as twin mortise-and-tenons. This will distribute the load over a wider area and reduce stress on the joint. If the design of a piece prohibits the use of large joints, use a number of smaller joints to spread the load and reduce stress.

• Make sure the elements of a joint are properly proportioned. If a tenon in a mortise-and-tenon joint is too thick, the mortise member will be weakened.

• When arranging the mating boards of a joint, always take into account the grain direction of the elements, and orient the pieces to compensate for wood movement.

• Cut the elements of a joint parallel to the grain. A tenon cut across the grain, for example, will not withstand shear and racking stress.

• For some joints, such as dovetails, use the completed part of the joint (the pins) to lay out the mating part (the tails) to reduce inaccuracies.

• Avoid laying out joints by eye; use the appropriate measuring and marking tools.

• If a joint requires reinforcement, use glue along with fasteners, dowels, biscuits, or splines.

APPROPRIATE JOINTS FOR WOOD TYPES

TYPE OF JOINT	SOLID WOOD	PLYWOOD	PARTICLEBOARD
Butt joints *(page 22)*			
Frame and case butt	Excellent (reinforce)	Good (reinforce)	Fair (reinforce)
Panel butt	Excellent	Poor	Poor
Edge butt	Excellent	Good (reinforce)	Fair (reinforce)
Face-to-face butt	Excellent	Excellent	Excellent
Scarf joint and pocket holes	Good (reinforce)	Not used	Not used
Butterfly joint	Excellent	Not used	Not used
Miter joints *(page 42)*			
Face miter	Good (reinforce)	Good (reinforce)	Good (reinforce)
Edge miter	Excellent (reinforce)	Good (reinforce)	Good (reinforce)
End miter	Good (reinforce)	Fair (reinforce)	Fair (reinforce)
Miter-and-spline	Excellent	Fair	Fair
Feather-spline	Fair	Poor	Poor
Coped joint	Good (reinforce)	Not used	Not used
Lap joints *(page 58)*			
Full lap, Half laps: T, mitered, dove-tailed, keyed dovetail, angled, cross, edge, half-blind, corner, glazing bar	Excellent (reinforce)	Fair	Fair
Rabbet joints *(page 60)*			
Rabbet, shiplap, stopped rabbet, mitered rabbet, double rabbet, dovetail rabbet	Good	Fair	Fair
Tongue-and-groove joints *(page 61)*			
Through tongue-and-groove, blind tongue-and-groove, glue joint	Excellent	Fair	Fair
Dado joints *(page 62)*			
Through, blind, and stopped dado	Good	Good	Fair
Dado-and-rabbet, tongue-and-dado, double dado	Good	Fair	Fair
Lock miter	Excellent	Good	Fair
Sliding dovetail, sliding half-dovetail, stopped sliding half-dovetail	Excellent	Not used	Not used
Mortise-and-tenon joints *(page 88)*			
Blind, haunched, angled, loose, round, twin, through, wedged through, pegged through, tusk, open	Excellent	Not used	Not used
Dovetail joints *(page 114)*			
Through, blind, half-blind, curved through, outlined through, box joint, half-blind box joint, finger joint	Excellent	Not used	Not used

BONDING WOOD

Over-tightening the clamps on a glue joint can squeeze out all the adhesive, resulting in a "starved" joint. Apply a thin, even layer of glue on the mating surfaces and stop tightening when a small bead of adhesive squeezes out of the joint.

Proper bonding of mating surfaces can be achieved in three steps: preparing the surface meticulously, applying the right type and amount of adhesive, and proper clamping.

First, the mating surfaces of a joint must be made as flat and smooth as possible with a jointer or hand plane. Rough surfaces have hundreds of tiny air pockets that can cause uneven gluing. Surfaces should also be clean; oil, sawdust, grease, and dirt can weaken a glue bond. Some oily woods, such as teak and rosewood, have extractives that inhibit the gluing process, but planing or jointing these woods just before glue-up removes most of the residue from the surfaces.

While glues made from organic materials such as fish glue and hide glue have been in use for centuries, most modern adhesives are derived from synthetic compounds. Glues such as resorcinol and epoxy cure by chemical reaction, while yellow and white glue cure by evaporation of the solvent they contain. Most glues seep into the wood, locking the wood fibers together and creating a bond that is stronger than the wood itself. To select the proper adhesive for your joinery tasks, see the chart opposite.

When applying glue, spread it evenly over both mating surfaces of the joint; it is better to apply a thin coat to both surfaces than a heavy coat to one. Avoid spreading glue with your fingers; a set of stiff-bristled brushes of different sizes can handle most gluing tasks. Some other applicators are shown below.

Joints should be clamped immediately after the adhesive is applied; position your clamps carefully to avoid cupping or bowing of the workpieces. Clamping presses the glue into a uniform thin film between the mating surfaces, while holding the pieces until curing takes place. See the back endpapers for a selection of clamps.

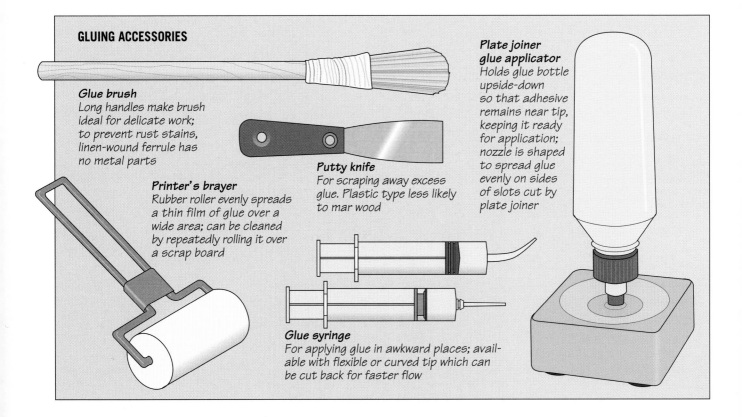

GLUING ACCESSORIES

Glue brush
Long handles make brush ideal for delicate work; to prevent rust stains, linen-wound ferrule has no metal parts

Printer's brayer
Rubber roller evenly spreads a thin film of glue over a wide area; can be cleaned by repeatedly rolling it over a scrap board

Putty knife
For scraping away excess glue. Plastic type less likely to mar wood

Glue syringe
For applying glue in awkward places; available with flexible or curved tip which can be cut back for faster flow

Plate joiner glue applicator
Holds glue bottle upside-down so that adhesive remains near tip, keeping it ready for application; nozzle is shaped to spread glue evenly on sides of slots cut by plate joiner

JOINERY ADHESIVES

TYPE	CHARACTERISTICS	USES
White glue	Polyvinyl-acetate based; not toxic or flammable • Strong bonding; working time 3 to 5 minutes • Setting time about 30 to 45 minutes; cures fully in 24 to 72 hours • Dries clear and colorless • Does not sand as well as yellow glue	General woodworking
Yellow glue	Aliphatic-resin based; not toxic or flammable • Better immediate adhesion for faster grab than white glue; working time 3 to 5 minutes • Setting time about 30 to 40 minutes; cures fully in 24 to 72 hours • Dries opaque (faded yellow); more heat-resistant for better sanding properties than white glue	General woodworking
Epoxy glue	Resin and hardener must be mixed prior to use; not flammable but may be toxic • Strong, waterproof bonding; working time 5 minutes to 2 hours (depending on type) • Setting time 5 minutes to 2 hours (depending on type); cures fully in 24 hours	Bonding acidic woods such as oak; use on exotic woods that bond poorly with other glues
Fish glue	Protein-based; not toxic or flammable • Average bonding; working time 60 to 90 minutes • Setting and curing time 12 hours • Sandable, dries an opaque color, resists solvents • Not water-resistant: Glue bond can be softened with water for disassembly	Furniture construction, luthier work, antique restoration and tasks that require a long working time
Hide glue	Protein-based; available in granular or liquid form; not toxic or flammable • Strong bonding, working time 3-5 minutes • Setting time 1 hour; cures fully in 24 hours • Sandable, dries a dark color • Not water-resistant, glue bond can be softened with water for disassembly	Cabinet construction, antique restoration, veneering, and fine woodworking
Casein glue	Milk-based, comes in powdered form; not toxic or flammable • Average bonding; working time 15 to 20 minutes • Setting time 15 to 20 minutes, cures fully in 8 to 12 hours • High resistance to water, dries an opaque color, sands cleanly, stains acidic woods	Oily woods that bond poorly with other glues, such as teak, yew, and lemonwood; laminating
Plastic resin	Urea-formaldehyde-based, available in powdered form; not flammable but toxic • Strong bonding, working time 20 minutes • Setting time 4 to 6 hours; cures fully in 3 days • Water resistance higher than that of aliphatic glues, does not stain acidic woods, sands cleanly	Veneering, laminating, and edge-gluing hardwood

REMOVING EXCESS GLUE

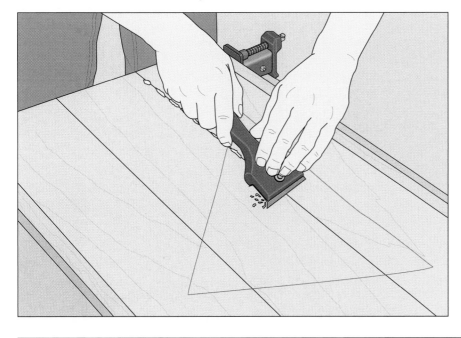

Scraping away adhesive
Once all your clamps have been tightened, use a putty knife to remove as much of the squeezed-out glue as possible after it sets but before it cures. The moisture from adhesive left on the surface will be absorbed by the wood, causing swelling and slowing drying time; hardened glue can also clog sandpaper, dull planer knives, and repel wood stain. Once the adhesive has dried, use a paint scraper to remove any squeeze-out that remains *(left).*

BUTT JOINTS

Of all the joints used to assemble boards, the butt joint is certainly the most straightforward. Affixing the edge, end, or face of one board to that of another may not always produce the strongest joint. However, a properly reinforced butt joint is an excellent option for dozens of woodworking tasks, from joining smaller boards into a wide panel to assembling carcases and frames.

The simple butt joint contains no interlocking parts, relying instead on the glue bond for its strength. The solidity of that bond is determined by the grain orientation of the mating boards. Gluing long grain to long grain, as in panel, edge, and face-to-face joints *(page 22)*, produces a solid connection, requiring no reinforcement. All other butt joints involve end grain; this porous surface provides a much less effective gluing surface than an equivalent area of long grain. Therefore, end grain joints must be reinforced.

Nails and screws can be used for reinforcement, but cabinetmakers try to avoid them for two principal reasons: Additional work is required to conceal the fasteners, and neither does as good a job joining end grain as some of the alternatives. Screws are considered superior for one application, however, and that is the task of fastening a tabletop to its supporting rails. The technique, which involves drilling angled pocket holes, is detailed on page 36.

The commercial jig shown above cuts accurate pocket holes with a minimum of setup time. With the workpiece clamped in the jig, the router-like cutter is pivoted into the face of the board to cut the pocket hole.

Most other joinery needs are filled by dowels, compressed-wood wafers or "biscuits," or splines, which can also serve to align parts of a joint that do not require reinforcement. Each demands mastery of a specialized technique—but the procedures are simple and they allow the quick assembly of strong, attractive joints in which the mechanical parts can be hidden from view.

At least one butt-joining technique—the butterfly key joint—is not meant to be hidden; in fact it is used as much for decoration as for strength. In this joint a double-dovetail key—the butterfly—is cut from a contrasting wood and used to tie together two edge-joined boards. The butterfly demands patience, but a well-set key can be a striking feature of a tabletop. The steps to making one are shown on page 39.

At the other end of the form-to-function scale is the use of threaded rods to reinforce such workaday surfaces as butcher blocks, workbenches, and countertops. These are often built up of face-glued stock, as shown on page 27, and the rods serve to stabilize the heavy slab when room humidity changes.

Doweling techniques are explained starting on page 28; biscuit joinery begins on page 32, and the correct use of splines is detailed on page 38.

Biscuits provide effective butt joint reinforcement. Here, the oval wafers are used to join the sides of a carcase. The glue causes the biscuits to expand in their slots, creating an exceptionally strong joint.

A CATALOG OF BUTT JOINTS

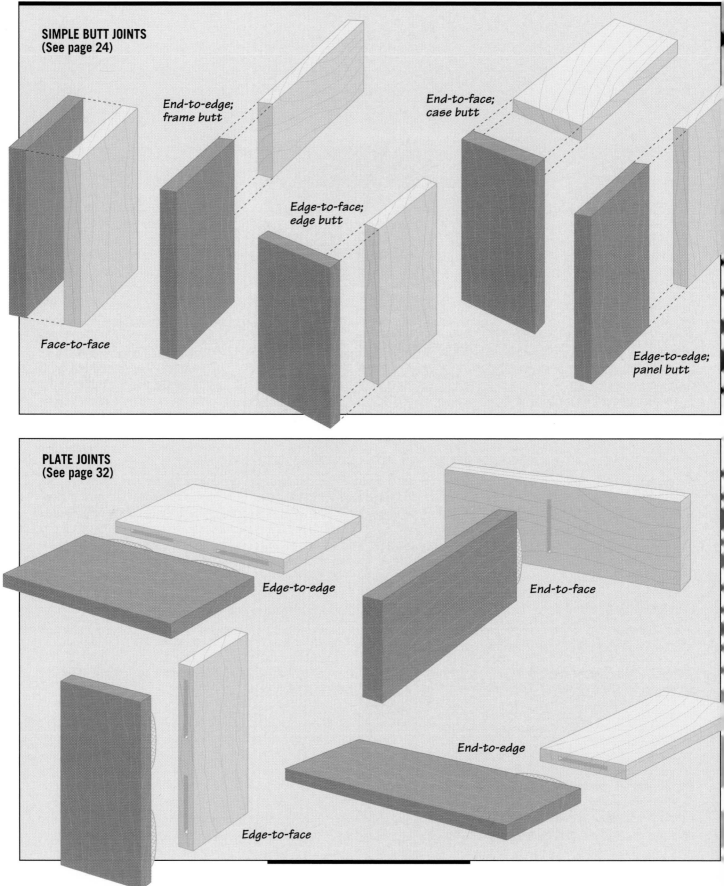

SIMPLE BUTT JOINTS
(See page 24)

End-to-edge;
frame butt

End-to-face;
case butt

Edge-to-face;
edge butt

Face-to-face

Edge-to-edge;
panel butt

PLATE JOINTS
(See page 32)

Edge-to-edge

End-to-face

End-to-edge

Edge-to-face

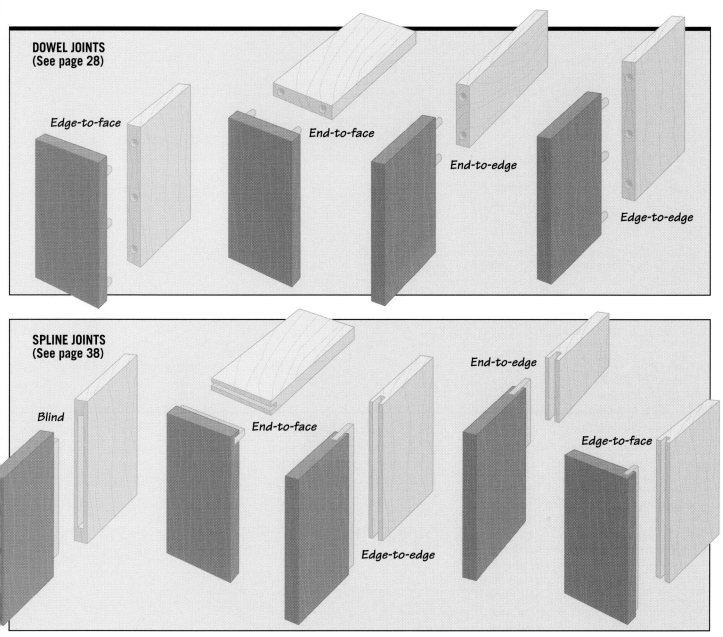

DOWEL JOINTS
(See page 28)

Edge-to-face

End-to-face

End-to-edge

Edge-to-edge

SPLINE JOINTS
(See page 38)

Blind

End-to-face

End-to-edge

Edge-to-edge

Edge-to-face

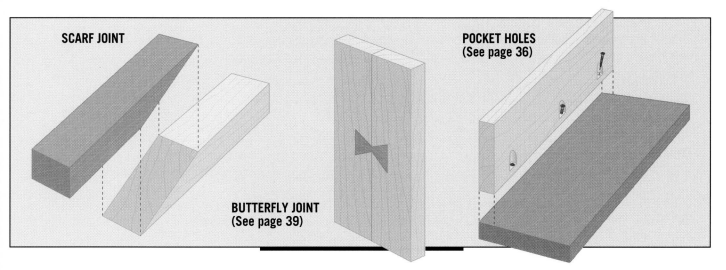

SCARF JOINT

BUTTERFLY JOINT
(See page 39)

POCKET HOLES
(See page 36)

MAKING BUTT JOINTS

Lumber is seldom available in planks wide enough for a tabletop or a carcase panel; sometimes it cannot be found thick enough for a specific task—a table leg, for example. Often, when you can find such stock, it is prohibitively expensive. To compensate for these shortcomings, woodworkers glue individual boards together. Panels are constructed from edge-to-edge butt joints, as shown below. Leg blanks are made by face gluing boards *(page 25)*. Provided the mating surfaces have been jointed smooth and square, and the proper gluing and clamping techniques are followed, the results are strong and durable. In fact, a well-assembled edge-to-edge or face-to-face butt joint pro-

vides a sturdier bond than the wood fibers themselves.

Before edge gluing boards, arrange the stock so the face of the panel will be visually interesting. The panel should create the illusion of a single piece

of wood rather than a composite. To minimize warping, most woodworkers arrange the pieces so that the end grain of adjacent boards faces in opposite directions *(page 25)*. Use a pencil to mark the end grain orientation on each board.

A jointer produces a smooth, straight, even edge. Gluing jointed boards together edge-to-edge will form a panel that is every bit as strong as a single piece of lumber.

EDGE GLUING

1 Applying the glue
Set two bar clamps on a work surface and lay the boards on top. Use as many clamps as you need to support the pieces at 24- to 36-inch intervals. Keep the bars upright by placing them in notched wood blocks. Arrange the stock to enhance its appearance, making sure the end grain of the boards runs in alternate directions. With the pieces butted edge-to-edge, mark a triangle on the stock to help you rearrange the boards at glue up. Next cut two protective wood pads at least as long as the boards. Leaving the first board face down, stand the other pieces on edge with the triangle marks facing away from you. Apply a thin glue bead to each edge *(right)*, then use a small, stiff-bristled brush to spread the adhesive evenly.

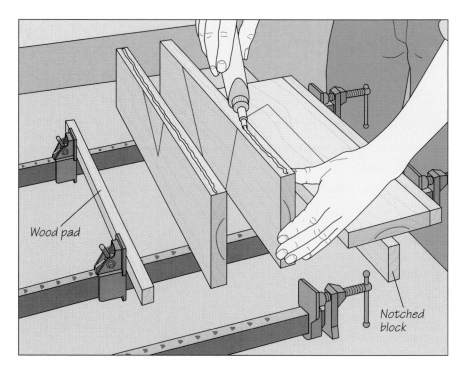

Wood pad

Notched block

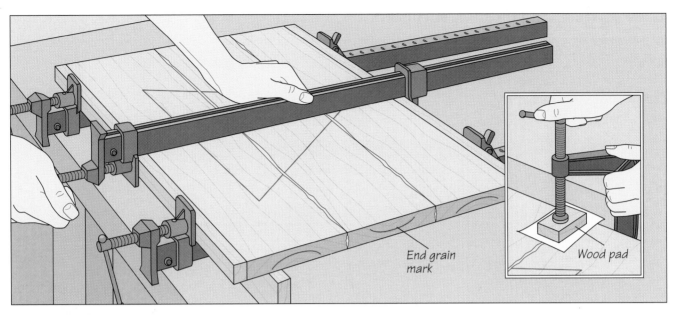

End grain
mark

Wood pad

2 Tightening the clamps

Set the boards face down and line up their ends, making sure the sides of the triangle align. Tighten the clamps under the boards just enough to press them together. Install a third clamp across the top center of the stock. Finish tightening the clamps *(above)* until there are no gaps between the boards and a thin bead of glue squeezes out of the joints. To level adjacent boards that do not lie perfectly flush with each other, use a C clamp and a wood pad centered over the joint near the end of the boards; use a strip of wax paper to prevent the pad from sticking to the boards. Then tighten the clamp until the boards are aligned *(inset)*.

FACE GLUING

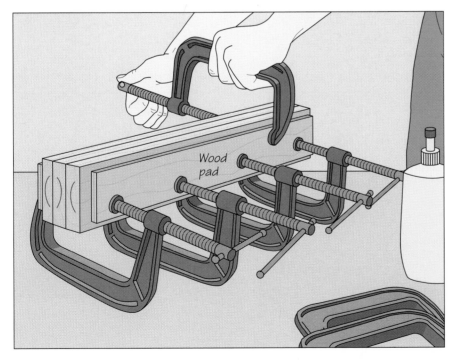

Wood
pad

Gluing up boards face-to-face

Cut your stock slightly longer and wider than necessary to enable you to square the blank if the boards shift during glue-up. Lay out the boards face-to-face, alternating the end grain of the pieces and arranging the stock to maximize grain and color. Spread glue on one mating surface of each joint, then use C clamps to hold the pieces together. Starting near the ends of the boards, space the clamps at 3- to 4-inch intervals; protect the stock with wood pads. Tighten the clamps just enough to press the boards together. Turn the assembly over so it sits on the first row of clamps and install a second row along the other edge *(left)*. Finish tightening all the clamps until there are no gaps between the boards and a thin glue bead squeezes out of the joints.

CLAMPING TECHNIQUES FOR THREE BUTT JOINTS

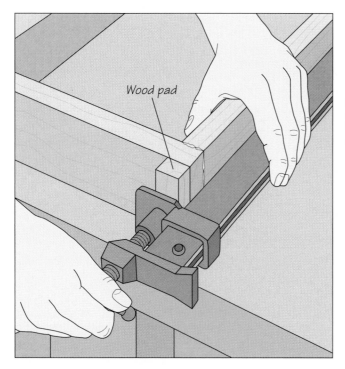

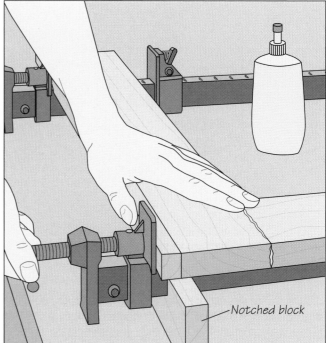

Gluing up a joint with end grain

Since both joints shown above involve gluing along end grain, you will need to reinforce the connection; use one of the methods presented later in this chapter, such as dowels, biscuits, or splines. Spread glue on the contacting surfaces, then use bar clamps to hold the joint together. For the case butt joint *(above, left)*, set the clamp on its side and the boards on edge on a work surface. Tighten the clamp as you hold the stock snug up against the bar and keep the joint square. For a frame butt joint *(above, right)*, set two bar clamps upright in notched wood blocks as you would for gluing up a panel *(page 24)*. (The second clamp serves to keep the boards level.) Lay the boards face down on the clamps, making sure the stock is well supported. Apply the adhesive, butt the pieces together, and tighten the clamps while holding the boards in alignment. For both setups, use wood pads to protect your stock.

Clamping an edge butt joint

Set two bar clamps on a work surface and lay the boards on top, one face down and one on edge. Use notched blocks and wood pads. Spread some glue on the mating edge and board face. Hold the upright piece flush against the bar while tightening the clamps a little at a time until adhesive squeezes out of the joint *(right)*. Install as many additional clamps as necessary between the first two to close any gaps between the boards.

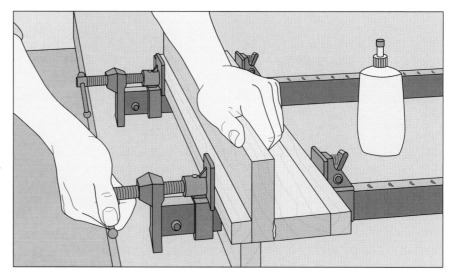

THROUGH BOLTS

Through bolts are an effective means of reinforcing workbench tops or butcher blocks made by face gluing boards. In addition to helping to align the boards, the bolts will reduce the possibility of splitting or warping as the wood's moisture content fluctuates from season to season.

REINFORCING BUTT JOINTS WITH THROUGH BOLTS

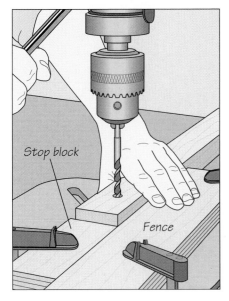

Stop block

Fence

Through bolt

Gluing up and bolting the panel

Mark three holes for the bolts on the face of one board, placing one a few inches from each end and one in the middle; center the marks between the edges. Install a bit in the drill press that is slightly larger than the bolts and align the bit with the middle mark. Clamp a stop block against the end of the board and a wood fence against its edge. Use this setup to drill the end holes in all the boards *(above, left)*. Use a similar setup to bore the middle holes. Counterbore the two face pieces to accommodate the nuts. Prepare the bolts by threading a nut on one end of each threaded rod; strike the end of each rod with a hammer and punch to jam the nut in place. Stand the front piece on edge and lay all the others face up on a work surface. Squeeze some glue on the boards and spread it evenly with a brush *(above, right)*. Press the board faces together, keeping their ends aligned. Feed the bolts through the holes, slip on the remaining washers and nuts, and give an initial tightening. Use bar clamps to press the boards together as in the photo above. Finish tightening the bolts with a socket wrench and add a third clamp across the top of the assembly.

DOWEL JOINTS

*Dowels can transform a weak butt joint into solid joinery.
In edge gluing* (right)*, the wooden pins help align the
boards. In frame* (above, left) *and case* (above, right) *butt
joinery, the dowels reinforce the relatively weak bond
between end grain and long grain. Dowel joints generally
hold up well to shear stress—when the pieces are being
pushed past each other; they are less effective at resisting
tension—when the pieces are being pulled apart* (page 15).

EDGE GLUING WITH DOWEL JOINTS

1 Marking the dowel holes
Arrange your stock on bar clamps as
for edge gluing *(page 24)*. Leaving one
board face down, stand the other pieces
on edge. To ensure that the dowels are
precisely centered, mark lines across the
edges of the boards—one about 4 inches
from each end and one in the middle. Then
adjust a cutting gauge to one-half the
thickness of the stock and use it to
mark the center of the edge at each
dowel location point *(right)*. The intersecting lines will accurately place the
dowels. For longer stock, you may want
to mark additional dowel holes.

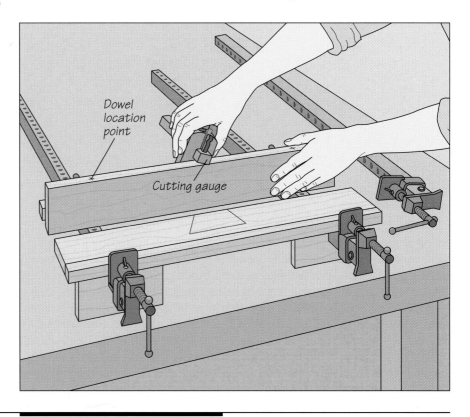

Dowel location point

Cutting gauge

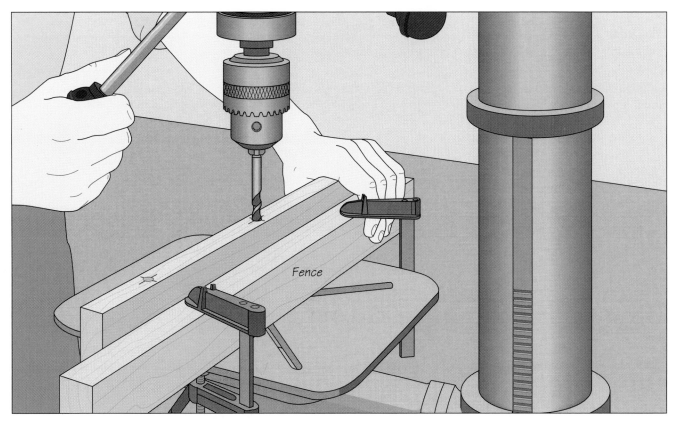

2 Boring the dowel holes
To avoid splitting your stock with the pins, use grooved dowels that are no more than one-half the thickness of the boards. Fit a drill press with a twist or brad-point bit the same diameter as the dowels, then set the drilling depth to $\frac{1}{16}$ inch more than one-half the length of the dowels. Clamp a fence to the drill press table to help keep the board edges perpendicular to the bit as you bore the holes. Then, holding the workpiece flush against the fence, position one marked point directly under the bit and bore the hole. Repeat to drill the remaining holes *(above)*.

SHOP TIP

Doweling jig
The commercial doweling jig shown here automatically centers dowel holes on the stock and spaces them at intervals you choose. Clamp the workpiece in handscrews, then secure the board to a work surface. Clamp the jig onto the edge of the stock. Fit your drill with a bit the same diameter as the dowels, then install a stop collar to control the drilling depth. Slide the rectangular bushing carrier along the jig, and insert the appropriate bushing to keep the bit square to the board. Holding the drill firmly, bore the hole.

BUILD IT YOURSELF

CENTER-DRILLING JIG

This simple jig will let you bore holes that are always centered on a board's face or edge. Cut the 18-inch arm from 2-by-2 stock. Mark the center of the top face of the arm and bore a hole for a guide bushing *(inset)*. The bushing should be slightly larger than the holes you plan to drill. Size the hole so the bushing will fit snugly, then press it in place.

Turn the arm over and mark a line down its middle. Mark points on the line roughly 1 inch from each end equidistant from the center, then bore a ⅜-inch hole halfway through the arm at each mark. Dab some glue in the holes and insert grooved dowels. They should protrude by about ⅜ inch. To use the jig, place it on the workpiece so that the dowels butt against opposite edges of the stock. Fit the drill bit into the bushing and bore the hole *(right)*.

For holes on a board edge, clamp the stock edge-up and set the jig on the stock with the dowels flush against opposite faces of the board.

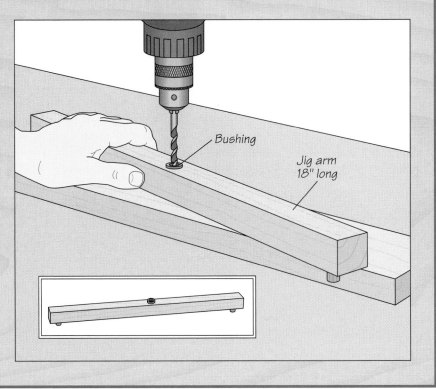

Bushing

Jig arm
18" long

3 Pinpointing the mating dowel holes
Insert dowel centers the same diameter as the dowels in each of the holes *(right)*, then lay the boards on the clamps with the triangle marks facing up. Align the marks and press the board edges together. The pointed ends of the dowel centers will pierce the edge of the adjacent board, providing starting points for the mating dowel holes. Bore these holes to the same depth as in step 2.

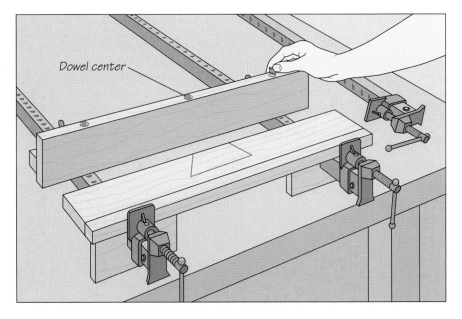

Dowel center

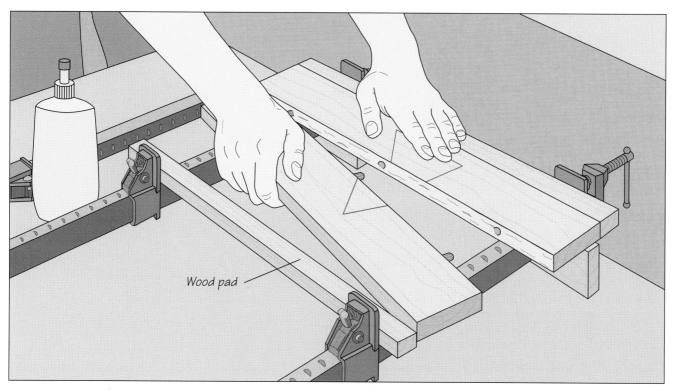

Wood pad

4 **Gluing up the boards**
Arrange the boards on bar clamps, using wood pads and notched blocks, as you would for edge gluing *(page 24)*. Apply a thin glue bead on the edges to be joined and spread it evenly. Use a stick to dab a small amount of adhesive in the bottom of each dowel hole. Do not spread glue directly on the dowels; the moisture will cause them to swell. Insert the dowels and use a hammer to tap them into final position. Avoid pounding, which can cause a board to split. Clamp the joint until the glue is cured.

SHOP TIP

Using a dowel to strengthen a butt joint
Screws do not hold well in end grain, so a fastener on its own is seldom strong enough to keep an end-to-face butt joint together. To reinforce the connection, bore a 3/8-inch-diameter hole vertically through the end grain piece about 1/2 inch from its end. Glue a dowel in the hole and let the adhesive dry. Then drive your screws through the mating piece into the dowel. The screws will be well anchored in the long grain of the dowel.

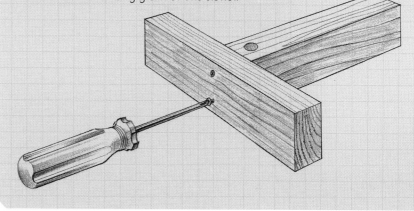

PLATE JOINTS

The plate, or biscuit, joint is strong and simple, although it requires the use of a specialized tool called a plate joiner, shown on page 33. The tool's retractable blade plunges into the mating boards, cutting semicircular slots that accept oval wafers of compressed beech. Once glue is added, the biscuits swell, creating a solid, durable joint—even in end grain. The slots are cut slightly larger than the biscuits, permitting a small margin of error while ensuring proper alignment.

EDGE GLUING BOARDS

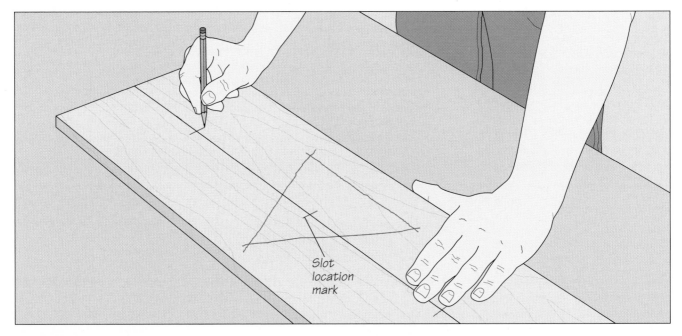

Slot
location
mark

1 Marking slot locations
Arrange the boards to be joined and mark a triangle on the surfaces as in edge gluing *(page 24)*. Then mark center lines for the slots across the board seams *(above)*. Start at least 2 inches in from each end and add a mark about every 8 inches.

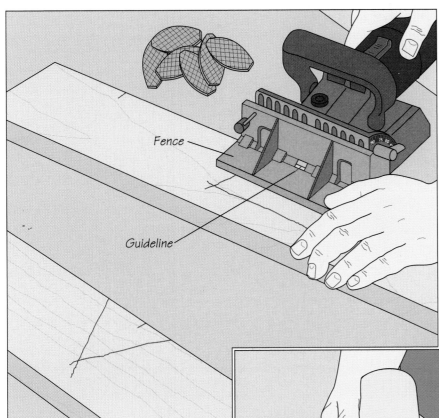

2 Cutting the slots

Set the plate joiner's depth of cut to suit the biscuits you are using and adjust the fence to center the slots in the board edges. Laying the fence on top of the stock, align the guideline on the faceplate with a slot location mark on the workpiece. Turn on the tool and plunge the blade into the board to cut the slot *(left)*. Repeat the procedure at the other slot location marks. With thin stock, the tool's base plate may touch the work surface, shifting the alignment of the slots. To prevent this, position the workpiece at the edge of the table so the base plate does not rest on the tabletop.

Fence

Guideline

3 Inserting the biscuits and gluing up the boards

Once all the slots have been cut, leave the last board face down and stand the others on edge with the slots facing up. Apply a bead of glue along the board edges and in the slots, inserting biscuits as you go *(right)*. (If you are working with long boards it is better to wait until all the adhesive has been applied before inserting the biscuits to prevent them from swelling before you have time to complete glue up.) The bottle shown in the illustration is specially designed to apply adhesive evenly on the sides of the slots; if you are using a standard glue bottle, spread the glue with a small wooden stick. Spread the adhesive evenly on the board edges, then fit the boards together quickly to prevent the biscuits from swelling prematurely. Hold the boards together with bar clamps as in edge gluing.

ASSEMBLING A CARCASE WITH PLATE JOINTS

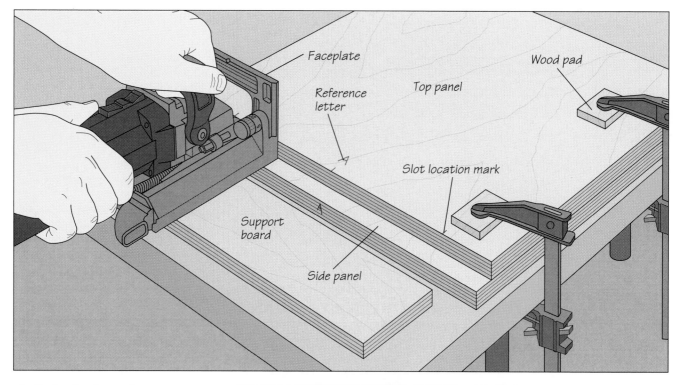

Faceplate

Reference letter

Top panel

Wood pad

Slot location mark

Support board

Side panel

A

1 Cutting the slots at the corners
With the setup shown here, you will be able to cut all the slots for one carcase corner without moving the panels. Set one of the side panels outside-face down and lay the top piece outside-face up on top of it, using reference letters to identify the carcase corners. Offset the top panel by the stock thickness, then clamp the pieces in place. Place a support board the same thickness as the stock in front of the panels, then mark the slot locations on the top panel. Setting the plate joiner on the support board, align the guideline on the faceplate with a slot location mark on the stock. Grip the joiner with both hands and cut the slot *(above)*. Repeat the process at the other marks and then, turning the plate joiner on end, align the guideline in the center of the tool's baseplate with a slot mark *(right)*. Push the tool down to cut the grooves in the side panel; repeat the clamping and cutting procedure for the other carcase corners.

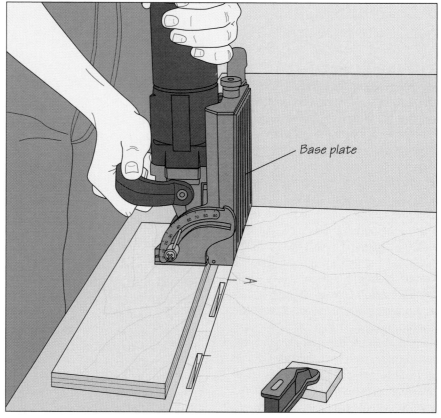

Base plate

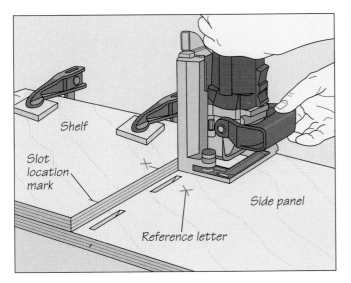

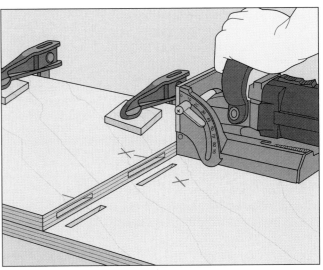

2 Cutting slots for a shelf

Mark slot location lines at both ends of the shelf. Mark lines across the inside face of both side panels where you wish to position the shelf, then set the shelf atop one side panel, aligning its edge with the reference line. Clamp the workpieces in place. Cut the slots in the panel by holding the tool's base plate against the shelf and aligning the guideline in the center of the plate with the location marks on the shelf *(above, left)*. Use the guidelines on the tool's faceplate to align and cut the slots in the shelf *(above, right)*. Reposition the shelf on the other side panel and repeat the procedure.

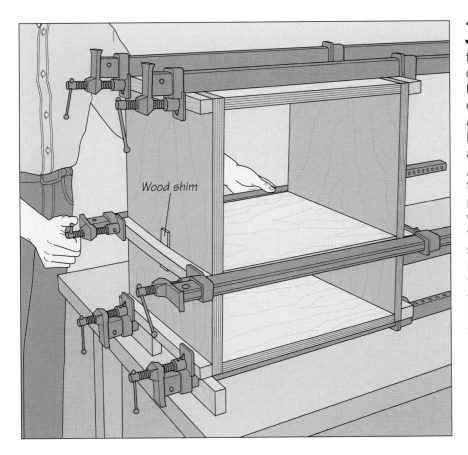

3 Gluing up the carcase

Once all the slots have been cut, set the panels and shelf on the work surface outside-face down. Apply glue and insert biscuits into their slots and along their edges as for gluing up boards *(page 33)*. Assemble the carcase, fitting the top and bottom panels and the shelf onto one side and then adding the other side *(see photo, page 20)*. Install two bar clamps across the top and bottom, using wood pads to protect the stock. Close the shelf joints with bar clamps at the front and back of the carcase, placing a ¼-inch-thick wood shim under each pad to maintain clamping pressure at the middle of the shelf. Tighten the shim clamps a little at a time until there are no gaps between the contacting surfaces and a small bead of glue squeezes out of the joints *(left)*.

POCKET HOLES

Pocket holes are commonly used with screws for attaching a tabletop to the supporting rails. Drilled at an angle, they solve the problem of having to screw straight through 3- or 4-inch-wide stock; they also conceal the fasteners. One of the many pocket hole jigs available, the model shown at right clamps the workpiece in position and features a bushing that keeps the drill bit at the correct angle. The combination bit shown bores a clearance hole for the screw shank and countersinks the hole for the head in one operation. A stop collar attached to the bit regulates the drilling depth.

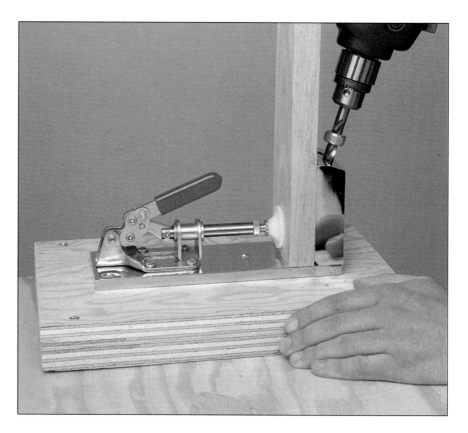

REINFORCING A BUTT JOINT WITH POCKET HOLES

Joining rails to a tabletop

Bore the pocket holes through the rails, using an electric drill with a commercial jig like the one shown above, or a drill press and a shop-made jig *(page 37)*. Space the holes about 4 inches apart. If you are using a drill with a special combination bit, the holes can be bored in a single operation. Otherwise, bore the holes in two steps with two different brad-point bits: Start with one slightly larger than the diameter of the screw heads, so they can be recessed as shown, and then bore the other a little larger than the screw shanks to allow for some movement. Once all the holes have been cut, set the tabletop face down on a work surface and mark lines on its underside to help you position the rails. Align a rail with one of the lines and drive the screws to attach the board to the top *(right)*. Repeat for the other rails.

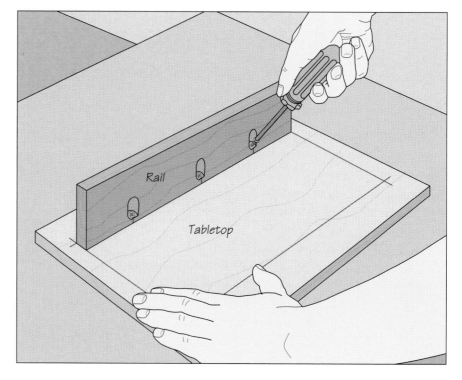

A POCKET HOLE JIG

To bore pocket holes on the drill press, use a pocket hole jig *(right)*, shop-made from ¾-inch plywood and two small pieces of solid stock. Refer to the illustration for suggested dimensions.

Screw the two sides of the cradle together to form an L. Then cut a 90° angle wedge from each support bracket so that the wide side of the cradle will sit at an angle of 15° from the vertical. Screw the brackets to the jig base, and attach the cradle on top of the brackets.

To use the jig, seat the workpiece in the cradle with the side to be drilled facing out and its top edge sitting in the V of the cradle. Bore the holes in two steps with two different bits as you would with an electric drill *(page 36)*. In this case, a Forstner bit and a brad-point bit are shown. The Forstner bit cuts a flat-bottomed hole ideal for recessing screw heads.

First, install the brad-point bit in the drill press and set the jig on the tool's table. With the machine off, lower the bit and position the jig to align the bit with the center of the bottom edge of the workpiece

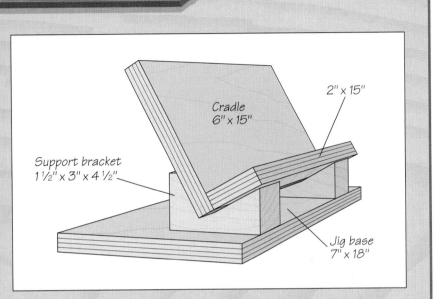

Cradle
6" x 15"

2" x 15"

Support bracket
1½" x 3" x 4½"

Jig base
7" x 18"

(below, left). Clamp the jig to the table and replace the brad-point with the Forstner bit.

Holding the workpiece firmly in the jig, feed the bit slowly to bore the

holes just deep enough to recess the screw heads *(below, right)*. To complete the pocket holes, reinstall the brad-point bit and bore through the workpiece.

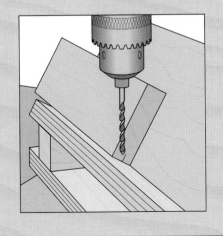

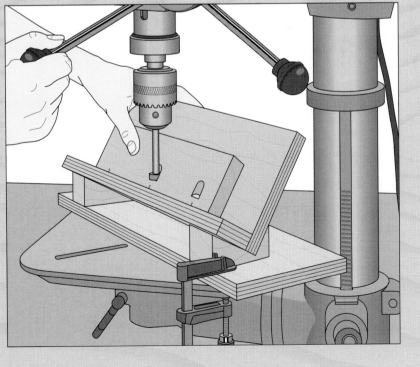

SPLINE JOINTS

Splines are thin strips of wood commonly used to align and reinforce butt joints, like the edge, case, and panel joints shown above (clockwise from top left). Made from plywood or solid wood no more than ⅓ the thickness of the stock, splines extend into grooves cut in both mating surfaces. Solid-wood splines should be cut with the grain running across their width, rather than lengthwise, to provide maximum strength. The width of the grooves should equal the thickness of the splines; their depth should be slightly more than one-half the width of the splines to allow for excess glue.

REINFORCING A BUTT JOINT WITH A SPLINE

Cutting grooves and inserting splines

Mark the thickness of the spline on the leading end of one board. Install a dado head of the appropriate width on the table saw and set the depth of cut. Align the marks on the workpiece with the dado head, then butt the fence against the face of the stock. To secure the workpiece during the cut, clamp a shim to the table and screw a featherboard on top. The shim will allow the featherboard to support the middle of the workpiece. Turn on the saw and feed the board into the dado head, keeping the workpiece firmly against the fence *(right)*. If you are working with narrow stock, use a push stick to complete the pass. Repeat the cut on the mating board, then spread some glue in the grooves, insert the spline, and clamp the boards as in panel *(page 25)* or edge butt gluing *(page 26)*. **(Caution: Blade guard removed for clarity.)**

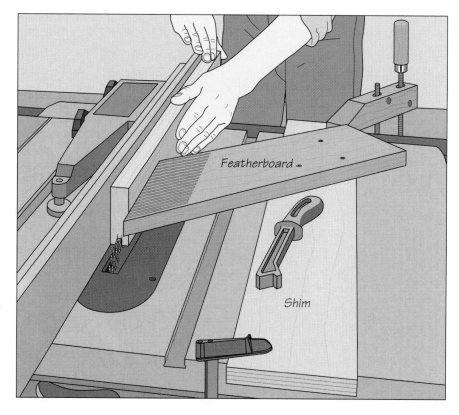

Featherboard

Shim

BUTTERFLY KEY JOINTS

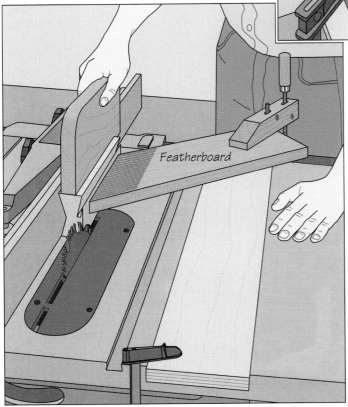

Also known as a double dovetail, the butterfly key joint serves to strengthen panel joints. If it is cut from a contrasting hardwood, the key adds a decorative element. There are several methods for making the joint, but here, the keys are fashioned on a table saw and the recesses for the keys are plowed with a router.

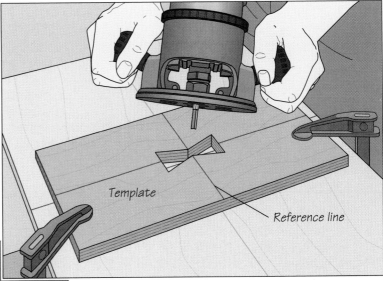

Template

Reference line

MAKING A BUTTERFLY KEY JOINT

Featherboard

Making a butterfly key joint

To make several keys, outline the double-wing shape on the end of your stock, making sure the grain runs along the length of the key rather than across its width. Adjust the blade angle on the table saw to 10°, align one of the key marks on the board with the blade and butt the fence against the stock. Support the workpiece with a featherboard set atop a shim. Make a rip cut on each side of the workpiece, then turn the board over and saw it twice more to cut out the butterfly pattern. Feed the stock with a push stick *(left)*. Cut individual keys from the board on the band saw. Rout the recesses for the keys using a template and a top-piloted straight bit. To make the template, outline one of the keys on a piece of plywood and cut out the pattern with a saber saw. Then mark intersecting reference lines for the location of the key on the panel and template. Clamp the template atop the stock, aligning the reference lines *(above)*, and rout the recess to a depth equal to the thickness of the key. Square the corners of the recess with a chisel. To glue in the key, spread adhesive in the recess and insert the key. Lay a wood pad across the panel, using clamps at its ends to hold the key in place while the glue dries.

MITER JOINTS

*A miter box is invaluable for making accurate angle cuts.
The commercial model shown above comes with its own
saw, a solid metal base, and legs that can be fastened down
to a work surface for added stability.*

Miters are among the commonest of joints. Builders use them when trimming around windows and doors; cabinetmakers usually miter carcase corners and picture frames because the miter conceals end grain. Although frames and boxes usually demand 90° corners, a miter joint may be any angle. All are equally simple to make, so long as the rules of mitering are followed: Each intersecting end must be cut exactly at one-half the total angle of the corner. Thus, the two pieces forming a 90° angle are cut at 45° each; those forming a 45° angle are cut at 22½°.

There are two types of miter joints: face miters and edge miters. Face miters *(page 45)* are cut across the faces of the pieces, and are often used to connect stiles and rails in frame-and-panel construction or join the members of a picture frame. Edge miters *(page 51)* can be made along the edges of the workpieces or across the end grain—also known as end miters or bevel miters. Because edge miters conceal the mating surfaces, they are used extensively in plywood carcase construction.

Miter joints are not only preferred for their clean lines. Because they offer more gluing area than ordinary butt joints, they are stronger. Still, any end-grain miter must be reinforced with splines, dowels, glue blocks, or biscuits.

Inserting splines is the method most commonly used to provide reinforcement *(page 48)*. Consisting of nothing more than strips of hardwood or plywood, splines are glued into grooves that are cut in both halves of a joint. The result is a strong, durable bond—even though its intention may be more decorative than functional, like the feathered spline demonstrated on page 49.

The angles of a miter joint can make it difficult to align during assembly; use special clamps and jigs like those illustrated on pages 50 and 55 to make the glue-up process easier. And, properly made, the reinforcements themselves can assure proper alignment.

Whether reinforced or not, the success of every miter joint depends on accurate cutting. The table saw miter jig on page 46 is designed to ease that task. But whether you are using a table saw, radial arm saw, or a backsaw with a miter box, careful measurement and proper setup will produce strong, attractive joints that will last for years.

*Making an octagonal carcase like the table support shown at
left calls for a series of identical bevel cuts. For the eight pieces
to fit properly, each edge must be cut at an angle of 22½° so
that the total of all the angles adds up to 360°.*

COMMON MITER JOINTS

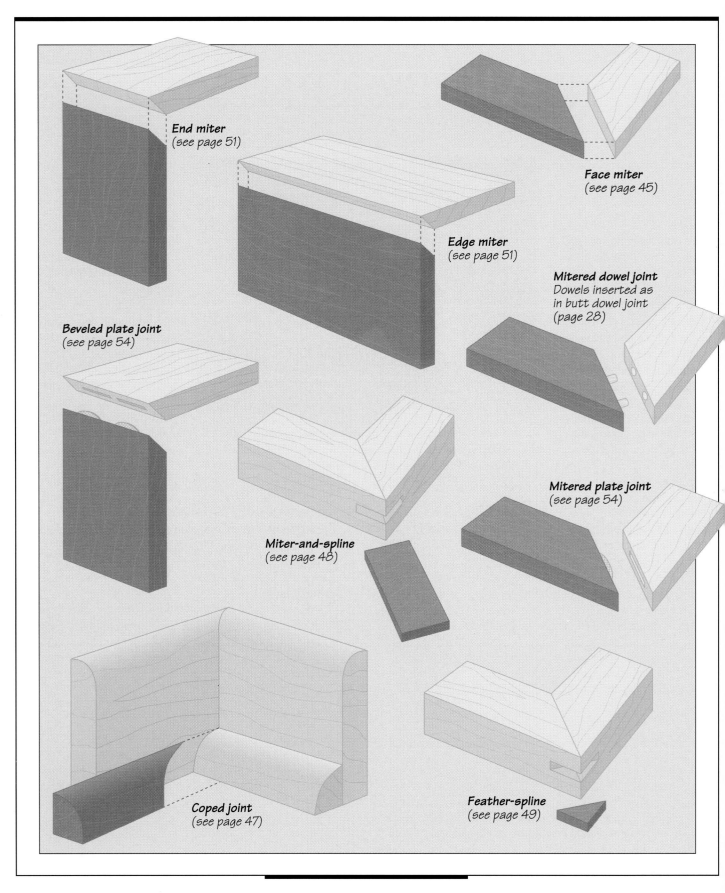

End miter
(see page 51)

Face miter
(see page 45)

Edge miter
(see page 51)

Mitered dowel joint
Dowels inserted as
in butt dowel joint
(page 28)

Beveled plate joint
(see page 54)

Mitered plate joint
(see page 54)

Miter-and-spline
(see page 48)

Coped joint
(see page 47)

Feather-spline
(see page 49)

JIGS AND ACCESSORIES

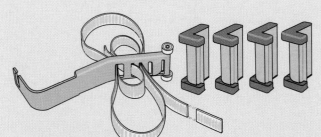

Web clamp set
For clamping carcases, especially those with beveled corners; includes brackets of various lengths to keep corners square

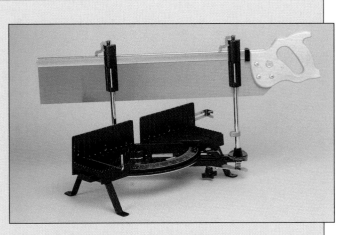

This commercial miter box, which comes with its own handsaw, can be adjusted to make a cut at any angle between 0° and 90°. For maximum convenience, the jig is fastened to a plywood base, which is then clamped to the work surface.

Picture frame clamp
Four-corner clamp used to assemble picture frames and other rectangular work; 2- to 48-inch clamping capacity

Corner clamp
Clamps miter joints up to 3 inches wide so that adjoining pieces are kept at right angles to each other; four clamps are required to glue up frame in one operation

Miter box
Used with a backsaw to cut miters and bevels. Model shown features slots for straight cuts, 45° miter cuts, and 45° bevel cuts; clamps at each end hold workpiece in place

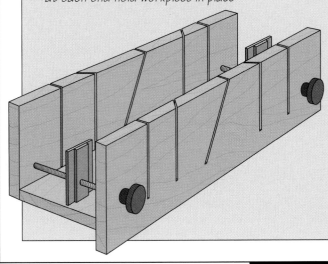

Web clamp
Also known as strap clamp; used to apply equal pressure around the circumference of a piece as when clamping a carcase assembled with several beveled pieces (page 40). Typically features a 1-inch-wide, 15-foot-long nylon strap with a ratcheting buckle, four corner brackets, and a wrench

MAKING MITER JOINTS

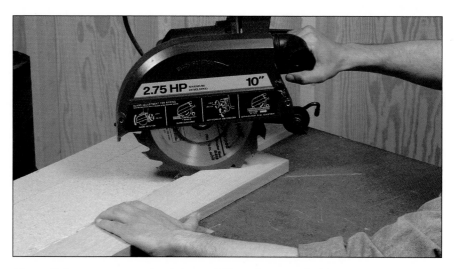

The radial arm saw cuts miter joints quickly and accurately. The arm that supports the motor and blade swivels to either side for face miter cuts. The motor can also be tilted for bevel cuts. Swiveling the arm and tilting the motor produces a compound cut.

Resist the temptation to cut miters freehand; the slightest error will result in gaps that are esthetically and structurally unsound. If you are making a standard 45° cut, use a combination square to set up your table saw or radial arm saw; or use a miter box with a backsaw. For a miter or bevel cut at any other angle, adjust your saw using a sliding bevel and a protractor. Make test cuts on a scrap board, then check your results. Through use, the slots in a wooden miter box can become out-of-square or too wide, resulting in a poorly fitting joint; you can achieve a good fit by sawing one half of a joint face up and the mating piece face down.

A MITER BOX

Cut three 15-inch-long pieces of hardwood or ¾-inch plywood for the base and the front and back pieces. Make the base wide enough for the stock you will be sawing. Rip the front and back pieces so that the depth of the box will be ½ inch less than the width of your backsaw blade from its teeth to the bottom of the spine. Cut the front piece 1 inch wider than the back piece to form a lip at the bottom of the box. Screw the front and back pieces to the base so that the top edges of the box are level. Use a combination square to mark cutting lines for the slots on the box's top edges. Lay out a 90° angle slot 3 inches from one end, and a 45° angle slot 3 inches from the other end. Outline a second 45° slot in the opposite direction between the first two slots. Make the cuts with a backsaw, using blocks clamped to either side of the cutting lines to guide the blade.

To use the box, secure the lip in a vise, then set the workpiece on the base, aligning the cutting line with the appropriate slot; clamp the board to the back piece. Start the cut by pulling the blade toward you a few times, then finish with push and pull strokes (left).

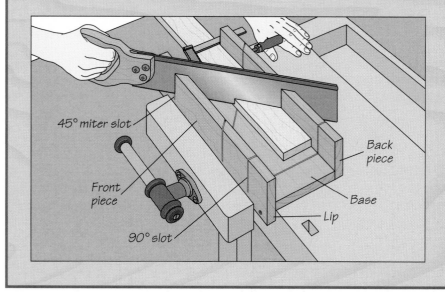

44

FACE MITERS

Face miter joints are a popular choice for picture frames; they hide end grain and direct the eye toward the center of the frame.

MAKING A FACE MITER JOINT

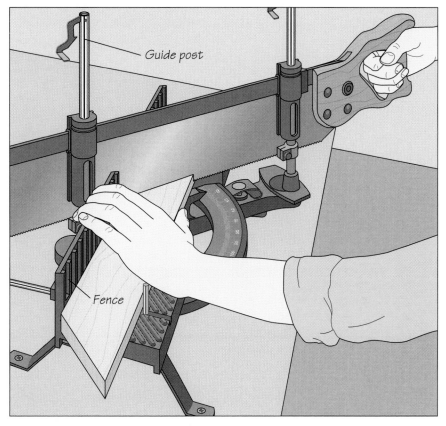

Guide post

Fence

1 Cutting the miter
To use the commercial miter box shown, secure the legs to a work surface. Swivel the saw assembly until the pointer indicates the miter angle you need; check the angle. Raise the saw assembly on the guide posts and slip the workpiece under the blade and on the base of the miter box. Align the cutting line with the blade and butt the board against the fence, then lower the blade onto the workpiece. Holding the stock firmly, make the cut as you would with a shop-made miter box *(above).*

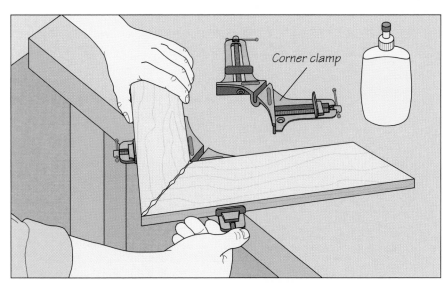

Corner clamp

2 Clamping the joint
Apply adhesive on the contacting surfaces of the joint. If you are using corner clamps for glue up, you will need an individual clamp for each corner of the frame. Fit adjoining boards in the clamps and tighten the two screws alternately until the joints are tight *(above).*

A MITER JIG FOR THE TABLE SAW

Making miter cuts on long, wide, or heavy workpieces can be tricky. The shop-built miter jig at right makes the task easier. Refer to the illustration for suggested dimensions.

Cut two 25-inch-long hardwood runners the same width as the saw's miter gauge slots. Bore clearance holes for screws into the undersides of the runners, 3 inches from each end and every 6 inches in between. Place the runners in the slots, then slide them out to overhang the back end of the table by about 8 inches. With the blade lowered below the table, position the jig base squarely on the runners, its edge flush with their overhanging ends; then screw the runners to the base, countersinking the screws. Slide the runners and the base off the front end of the table and drive in the remaining screws. Attach the back support piece along the rear edge of

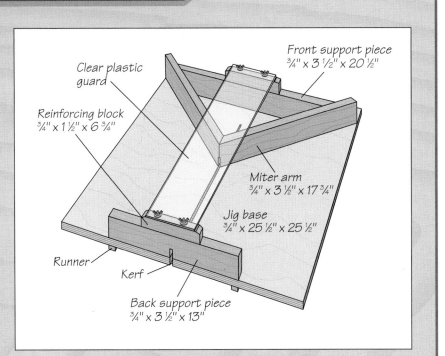

Front support piece
¾" x 3 ½" x 20 ½"

Clear plastic guard

Reinforcing block
¾" x 1 ½" x 6 ¾"

Miter arm
¾" x 3 ½" x 17 ¾"

Jig base
¾" x 25 ½" x 25 ½"

Runner

Kerf

Back support piece
¾" x 3 ½" x 13"

the jig, centered between the runners. Then, with the runners in the miter gauge slots, raise the blade and make a cut through the support piece and three-quarters of the way across the base. Turn off the saw and lower the blade. Next, place the miter arms at 90° to each other in the middle of the jig, centered on the kerf. Screw the arms and the front support piece in place. Attach the reinforcing blocks to the support pieces and fasten a clear plastic blade guard to the blocks with hanger bolts, washers, and wing nuts.

To use the jig, fit the runners into the miter gauge slots. Slide the jig toward the back of the table until the blade enters the kerf. Butt the workpiece against the left arm of the jig, align the cutting line with the saw blade, and clamp a stop block to the arm at the end of the board. Cut the miter, holding the workpiece firmly against the arm and stop block *(left)*. Make the mating cut the same way using the right arm of the jig.

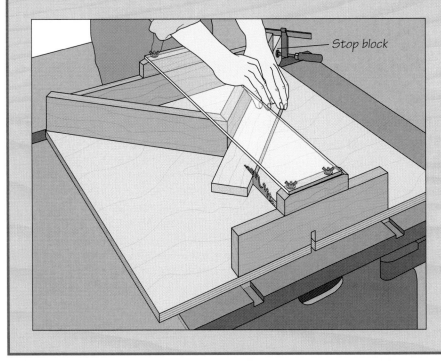

Stop block

COPED JOINTS

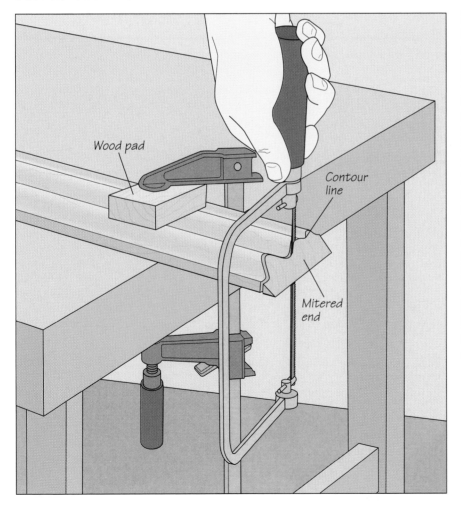

Coped joints are often used to connect two pieces of contoured molding at inside corners. They are superior to standard miters for concealing slight inaccuracies in the fit of the pieces. Coping is a two-step operation. First, a standard 45° bevel cut is made at the end of one piece. This reveals a contour line, which can then be followed with a coping saw.

CUTTING A COPED JOINT

Wood pad

Contour line

Mitered end

Coping contoured molding

Cut the end of a piece of molding at a 45° angle to reveal the contour line on the face. To make the coped cut, clamp the molding face-up on a work surface, protecting the workpiece with a wood pad. Install a narrow blade on a coping saw, making sure that the teeth are facing the handle so that the saw cuts on the pull stroke. Cut along the contour line carefully with the saw blade held perfectly upright *(left)*. For a tight fit, undercut the joint slightly, so that only the front of the board contacts the face of the mating piece. If the blade binds in the kerf, make occasional release cuts into the waste to let small pieces fall away. Position the coped end against the face of the mating piece to test the fit. Smooth out any slight irregularities with a round file or fine sandpaper wrapped around a dowel.

MITER-AND-SPLINE JOINTS

The miter-and-spline is basically a face miter with a spline glued into grooves cut in the mitered ends. For maximum strength, the spline should be cut so that its grain runs across its width, rather than lengthwise, or be made from plywood.

ROUTING A MITER-AND-SPLINE JOINT

Cutting the grooves

Make the 45° miter cuts in each work-piece first. Install a three-wing slotting cutter in your router and mount the tool in a table. Position the fence in line with the bit pilot, then place the workpiece flat on the table and center the bit on the edge of the stock. Feed the workpiece into the cutter with a miter gauge, hold-ing the edge of the board flush against the gauge and one mitered end flat against the fence *(right)*. (You can also rout the grooves for miter-and-spline joints by using a straight bit and feeding the stock on end into the bit.) Once all the grooves have been made, cut a spline for each joint; make it twice as wide as the depth of the groove, less 1/32 inch for clearance. Glue up the joint as you would a standard miter *(page 45)*, spreading glue in the grooves.

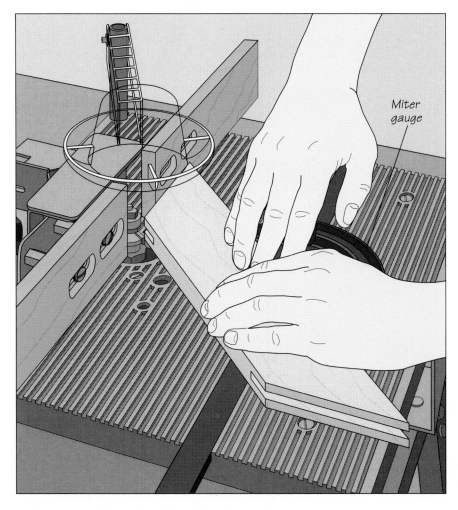

Miter gauge

FEATHER-SPLINE JOINTS

The spline in a feather-spline joint serves more of a decorative role than a structural one. In contrast to the miter-and-spline, the groove for the feather spline is cut after the corner is glued up.

MAKING A FEATHER-SPLINE JOINT

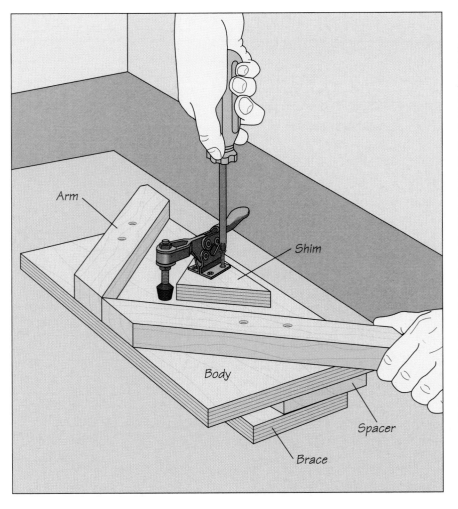

Arm

Shim

Body

Spacer

Brace

1 Making the jig
You can cut the grooves for a feather-spline joint on the table saw using the fence-straddling jig shown at left. The jig feeds the corner of a mitered frame across the table and squarely into the blade. Cut the body and brace from ¾-inch plywood and the arms from 1-by-2 stock. Make the body, spacer, and brace about 16 inches long and the arms 12 inches long; the body should be about 5 inches wide. (The thickness of the spacer and the width of the brace depend on the dimensions of your saw's rip fence.) Attach the spacer to the body and the brace to the spacer so the jig slides freely along the fence without wobbling. To prepare the arms, cut 45° miters at both ends and screw them to the body so that they are perpendicular to each other; check that the joint between them forms a 90° angle. To complete the jig, screw a shim to the body and fasten a toggle clamp to the shim *(left)*. Make certain there are no screws close to the bottom of the jig where the blade could strike one.

2 Cutting the grooves

To use the jig, place it astride the fence and position the two so the cut will be made in the middle of the workpiece. Slide the jig along the fence to cut grooves through the mitered ends of the arms. Turn off the saw and pull the jig back to the front of the table. Seat the frame in the jig so a corner is butted against the center of the V formed by the arms and clamp the workpiece in place. Feed the stock into the blade *(right)*, holding the jig with both hands. Cut triangular splines to fit in the grooves. Spread a little glue in the grooves and insert the splines. Once the glue has cured, cut and sand the projections flush with the frame.

BUILD IT YOURSELF

MITER CLAMPING BLOCKS

You can glue up mitered corners without special clamps, instead using handscrews and the special blocks shown at right. You will need one clamp and two blocks for each corner. Use stock the same thickness as your workpiece for the blocks; on one edge, cut the 45° angle and the V-shaped notch *(inset)*.

To use the blocks, apply glue to the contacting surfaces and press them together. At each corner, use string to tie the blocks snugly to the edges of the frame, securing the loose end in the notch. Set the jaws of the handscrew against the 45° angle edges of the blocks and tighten the clamp *(right)* until there are no gaps between the mitered ends and a thin bead of glue squeezes out of the joint. To keep the frame square, tighten the handscrews a little at a time, checking the corner with a combination square.

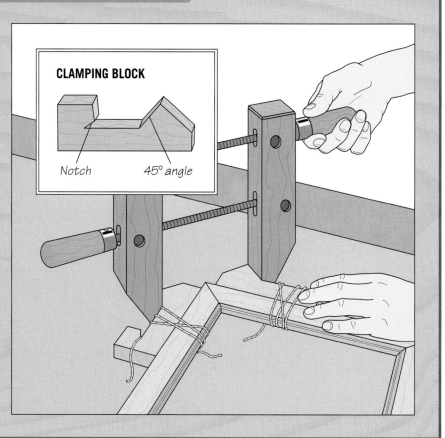

CLAMPING BLOCK

Notch   45° angle

EDGE MITER JOINTS

Edge miter joints feature matching bevel cuts in the mating pieces, either across the workpiece end (below) *or along the edge* (far right). *The edge miter is a popular joint for carcase corners because it conceals end grain. Both examples shown are reinforced with splines.*

CUTTING AN EDGE MITER JOINT

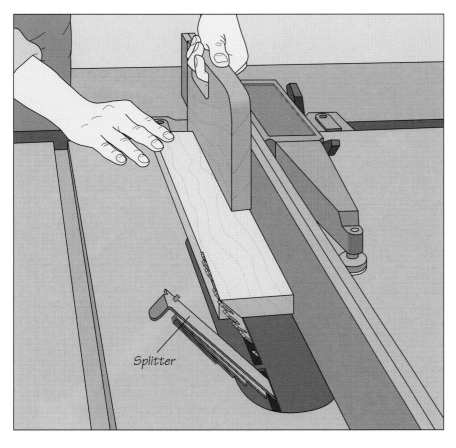

Splitter

Making the bevel cut

To cut a standard edge miter joint on the table saw, set the blade angle at 45° and position the rip fence for the width of cut, ensuring that the blade teeth are pointing away from the fence. Raise the splitter to keep the kerf open while the cut is being made, which will prevent binding and kickback. Feed the workpiece into the blade, using a push stick to keep the board flat on the saw table *(left)*. **(Caution: Blade guard removed for clarity.)** To cut the bevel across the end of a board, move the fence aside and feed the workpiece into the blade with the miter gauge. Once all the bevel cuts have been made, reinforce the joints with splines *(page 52)*, glue blocks *(page 53)*, or biscuits *(page 54)*.

REINFORCING EDGE MITERS WITH SPLINES

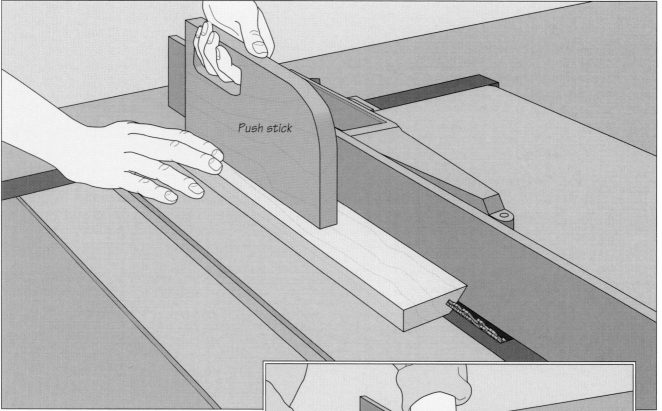

Push stick

Cutting the grooves on a table saw

Install a dado blade, adjusting it to cut a groove the same width as the thickness of your splines—often ¼ inch. Set the blade angle at 45° and make the cutting depth slightly more than one-half the width of the splines—often ¾ inch. Align the mitered edge of the workpiece with the dado head so the groove will be closer to the inside corner of the joint to ensure that the cut will not penetrate the top face of the board. Butt the rip fence against the workpiece. With the saw unplugged, rotate the dado head by hand to make certain that it clears the fence. If not, attach an auxiliary wood fence, reposition the rip fence accordingly, and make a relief cut. Cut the groove as you would a bevel, using a push stick to apply pressure on the table *(above)*. To cut a groove across beveled end grain, set up the dado head and fence as you would for a cut along the edge. Then feed the workpiece with the miter gauge *(right)*, keeping the board flush against the gauge and the fence. Fashion splines and glue up the joint as you would a miter-and-spline joint *(page 48)*.

Miter gauge

Routing grooves

You can also cut the grooves for a spline-reinforced edge miter using a router fitted with a commercial edge guide. Secure the mating pieces in a vise, beveled surfaces facing out, making sure that their ends and edges are flush. Install a straight bit as thick as your splines and set the cutting depth at slightly more than one-half the spline width. Attach an edge guide on the router and align the bit over one of the beveled edges so the groove will be closer to the inside corner of the joint. Then butt the guide fence against the other beveled edge and fix it in place. Rout the groove by riding the base plate flat on the edge to be cut while pressing the guide fence against the mating piece. Turn the router around and repeat the cut in the other piece *(right)*.

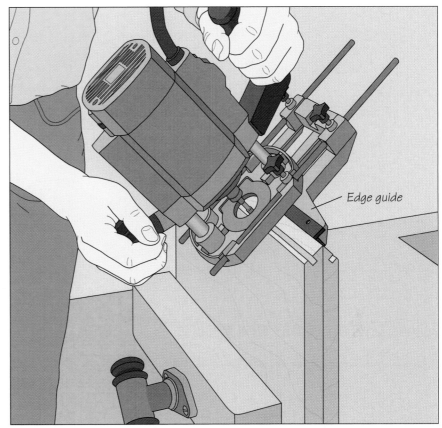

Edge guide

REINFORCING EDGE MITERS WITH GLUE BLOCKS

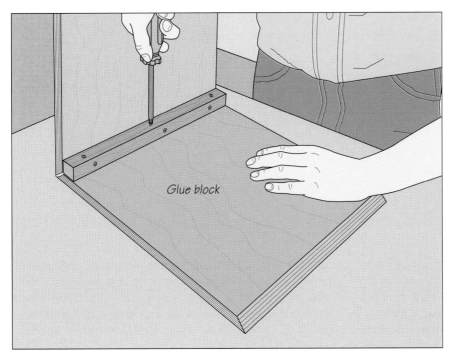

Glue block

Making and attaching glue blocks

Use 1-by-1 stock as long as the joint. Before assembling the carcase, screw a block to one piece, aligning the edge of the block with the inside edge of the bevel. Spread glue on the beveled surfaces, press the boards together, then attach the block to the other piece *(left)*. Repeat with the remaining corners of the carcase, using bar clamps if necessary to hold the assembly square.

MITERED PLATE JOINTS

Plate joinery is a simple way to fasten boards or panels together, whether the joining surfaces are mitered or beveled. Once glue is added, the biscuits swell, creating a strong, durable joint.

JOINING BEVELED CORNERS WITH BISCUITS

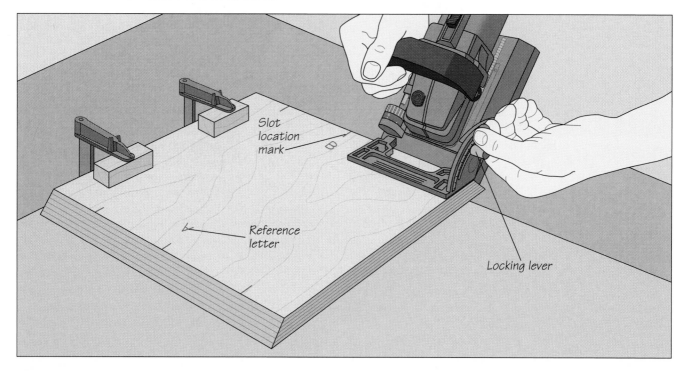

Slot location mark

Reference letter

Locking lever

1 Setting up the plate joiner
Place two adjacent panels on a work surface, inside-face up, and mark slot locations on both pieces; also add reference letters for ease of assembly. Start about 2 inches in from the edges, spacing the lines at 4- to 8-inch intervals. Repeat the procedure at the other three corners of the carcase. Adjust the plate joiner's fence to the proper angle, following the manufac- turer's directions. For the model shown, the panel is clamped to the work surface with one beveled end projecting off the edge. Rest the tool's faceplate against the end, loosen the fence locking lever and swivel the fence downward against the face of the panel. Lock it in place while the faceplate is flush against the bevel *(above)*.

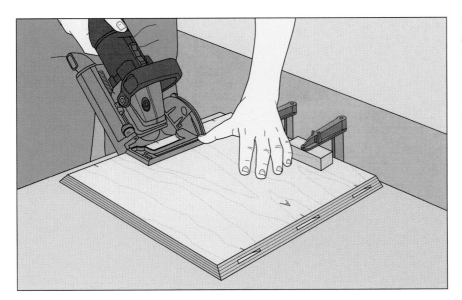

2 Cutting the slots

Holding the tool firmly against the stock, align the guideline on the face-plate with a slot location mark. Switch on the tool and plunge the cutter into the workpiece *(left)*. Repeat the procedure to cut the remaining slots.

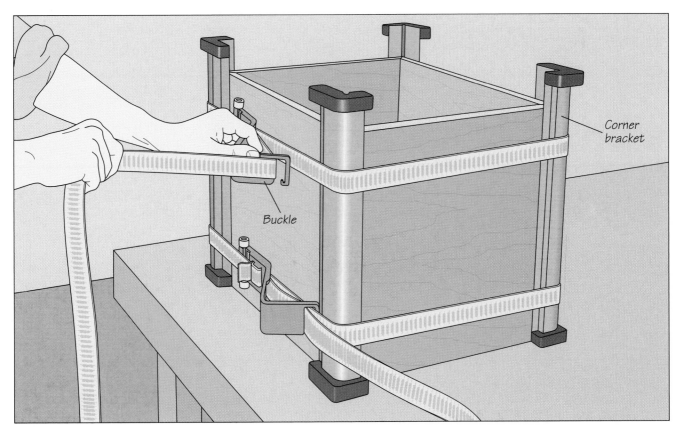

Corner bracket

Buckle

3 Gluing up the carcase

Once all the slots have been cut, set the panels on the work surface inside-face up. Squeeze glue into the slots and along the edges of the panels, inserting biscuits as you go. Assemble the carcase, working quickly to prevent the biscuits from swelling before you have had time to complete the glue up. To keep the beveled edges from slipping out of alignment as the adhesive is drying, secure the carcase with web clamps. The type shown here uses corner brackets to distribute pressure evenly along the length of each joint. Wrap straps around the unit and tighten them with the buckles before locking them in place *(above)*.

LAP, RABBET, GROOVE, AND DADO JOINTS

Shelves are often fixed to carcase sides with dado joints. Here, a router plows a through dado. An edge guide helps keep the cut parallel to the end of the panel.

The three dozen joints featured in this chapter are used in applications as varied as building cabinet carcases and piecing together frames and doors. This is a versatile family of joints, with the added virtue of being strong and simple.

In addition, almost all of these joints can be made in several ways, using either hand or power tools. For example, a dado can be cut with a router, a table saw, or a radial arm saw; it can be started with a hand saw and finished with a chisel. However, the typical woodworker will probably produce better-fitting joints in less time using power tools.

Perhaps the simplest of all joints are lap joints, the first covered in this chapter. As the name suggests, a lap joint is formed by laying one board over another and fastening the two at the required angle. The simple lap is weak and unattractive, but the joint can be rendered strong and elegant by first cutting a dado in one or both boards so that their faces lie flush with each other. The lap provides good long-grain surface contact for gluing, and additional reinforcement is seldom required unless the joint will be subjected to tensional stress.

Rabbet joints, the second group described, are most frequently used to join carcase and drawer corners, and less often for edge joining. Some variants, like the stopped rabbet *(page 75)* and the mitered rabbet *(page 76)*, are intended to conceal the end grain of the pieces. Remember, however, that any corner joinery that mates end grain requires reinforcement in the form of dowels, screws, or glue blocks.

A third group, tongue-and-groove joints, are most often used for edge-to-edge joinery. They may be glued, but sometimes are assembled dry so that the wood can move as humidity alters the moisture content.

Dado joints, illustrated at left and on the opposite page, are simple and useful; they are the method of choice for installing shelves or assembling drawers. A self-locking joint can be made by adding a dovetail.

A catalog of lap, rabbet, groove, and dado joints begins on page 58; a section on techniques for making them begins on page 64. Experiment with the methods shown, or alter them to suit your own skills and the tools you own. The results should be useful and enlightening.

The dado joint is a popular choice for assembling drawers. The dado-and-rabbet works well for joining the back to the sides, while the drawer front demands a stronger joint such as a double dado.

LAP JOINTS

The lap, rabbet, tongue-and-groove, and dado joints illustrated on the following pages appear quite different, but all are linked by a common feature: Each owes its strength to a channel of some sort in one piece that accepts a mating piece. Some joints, like the dovetailed half-lap *(page 69)*, are essentially variations on a theme, introducing a decorative effect or a slight modification that adds an extra measure of strength. Others solve a particular problem; for instance, the glazing bar half-lap *(page 70)* connects the muntins of a window sash or a glazed door.

Most of the techniques shown on the following pages can be applied to make other joints shown in the chapter when a similar type of cut is needed. For example, the handsaw and chisel technique shown on page 68 can be used to make a dado, end rabbet, or lap cut; a backsaw and edge guide clamped onto the workpiece can take the place of a miter box.

LAP JOINTS

T half-lap joint
Identical to cross half-lap joint (page 66), except one or both pieces intersect between ends, rather than at ends

Mitered half-lap joint
Similar to corner half-lap (page 64); cheek of one piece and shoulder of mating board are mitered at 45°

Full lap joint
Dado in one piece is deep enough to house full thickness of mating board; dado is cut as in cross half-lap (page 66)

ANATOMY OF A CORNER HALF-LAP JOINT
(See page 64)

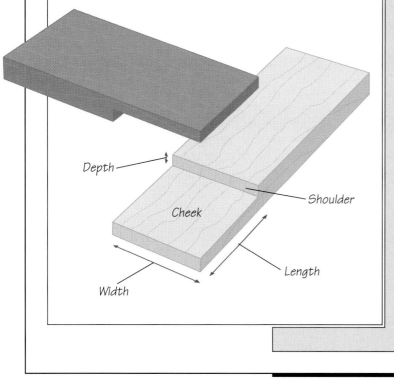

Depth

Cheek

Shoulder

Length

Width

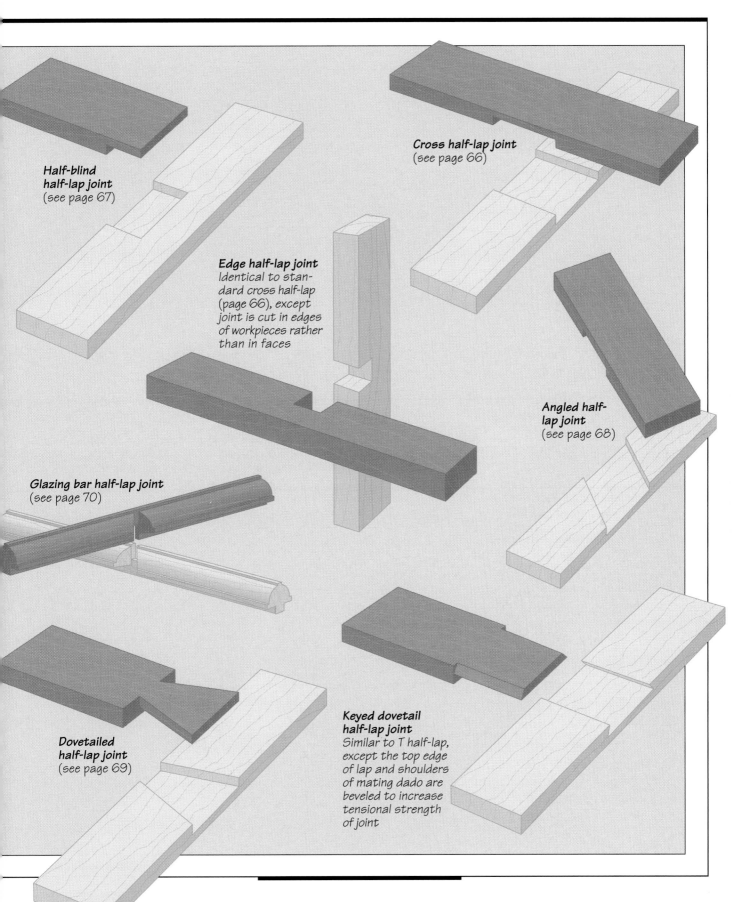

**Half-blind
half-lap joint**
(see page 67)

Cross half-lap joint
(see page 66)

Edge half-lap joint
Identical to standard cross half-lap
(page 66), except joint is cut in edges
of workpieces rather than in faces

Angled half-lap joint
(see page 68)

Glazing bar half-lap joint
(see page 70)

**Dovetailed
half-lap joint**
(see page 69)

**Keyed dovetail
half-lap joint**
Similar to T half-lap, except the top edge
of lap and shoulders of mating dado are
beveled to increase tensional strength
of joint

RABBET JOINTS

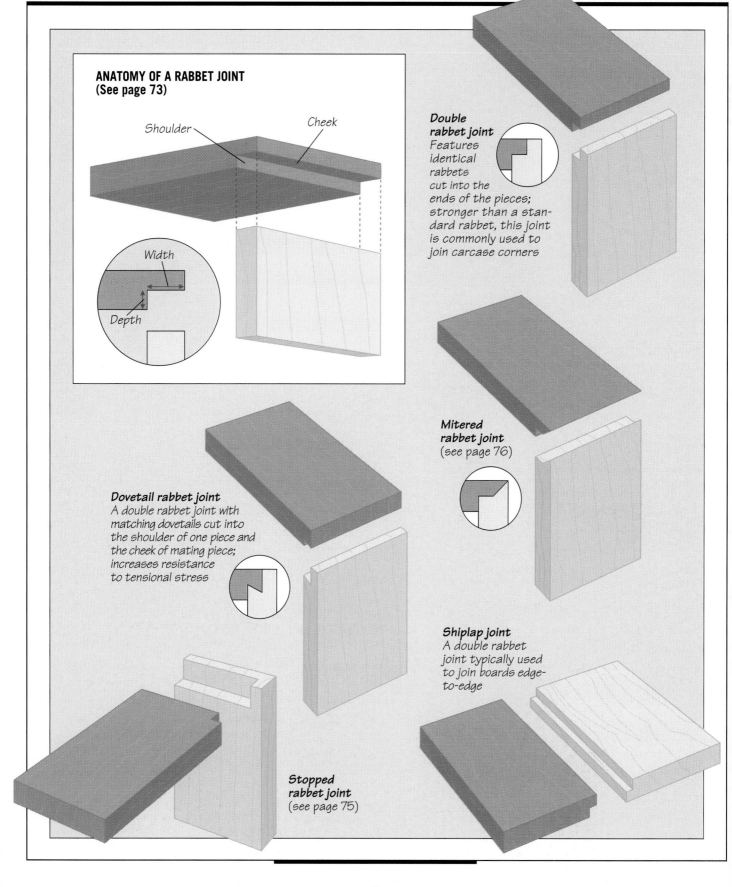

ANATOMY OF A RABBET JOINT
(See page 73)

Shoulder

Cheek

Width

Depth

Double rabbet joint
Features identical rabbets cut into the ends of the pieces; stronger than a standard rabbet, this joint is commonly used to join carcase corners

Mitered rabbet joint
(see page 76)

Dovetail rabbet joint
A double rabbet joint with matching dovetails cut into the shoulder of one piece and the cheek of mating piece; increases resistance to tensional stress

Shiplap joint
A double rabbet joint typically used to join boards edge-to-edge

Stopped rabbet joint
(see page 75)

TONGUE-AND-GROOVE JOINTS

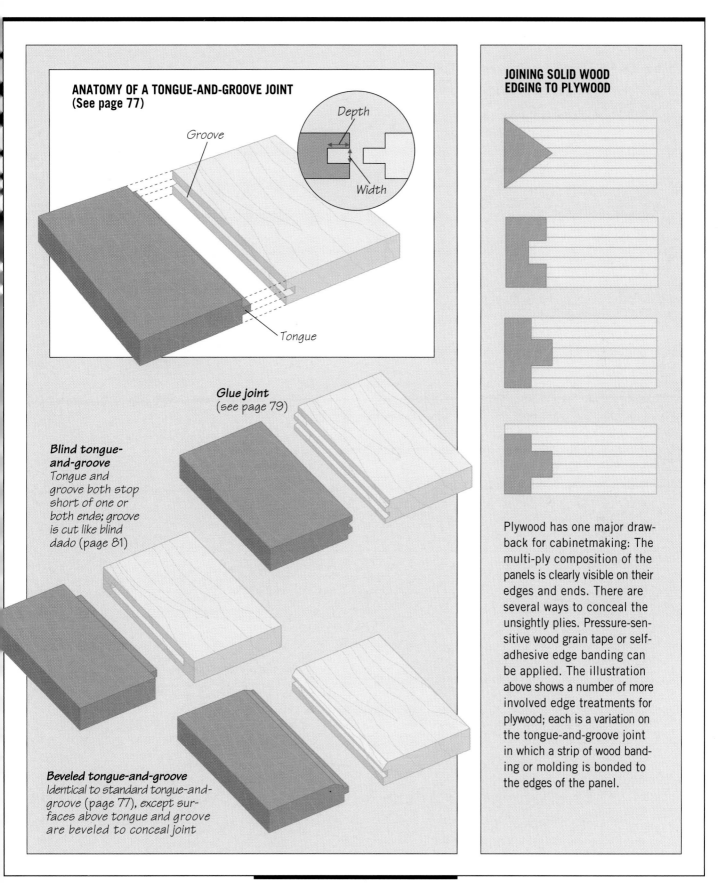

ANATOMY OF A TONGUE-AND-GROOVE JOINT
(See page 77)

Groove

Depth

Width

Tongue

Glue joint
(see page 79)

Blind tongue-and-groove
Tongue and groove both stop short of one or both ends; groove is cut like blind dado (page 81)

Beveled tongue-and-groove
Identical to standard tongue-and-groove (page 77), except surfaces above tongue and groove are beveled to conceal joint

JOINING SOLID WOOD EDGING TO PLYWOOD

Plywood has one major drawback for cabinetmaking: The multi-ply composition of the panels is clearly visible on their edges and ends. There are several ways to conceal the unsightly plies. Pressure-sensitive wood grain tape or self-adhesive edge banding can be applied. The illustration above shows a number of more involved edge treatments for plywood; each is a variation on the tongue-and-groove joint in which a strip of wood banding or molding is bonded to the edges of the panel.

DADO JOINTS

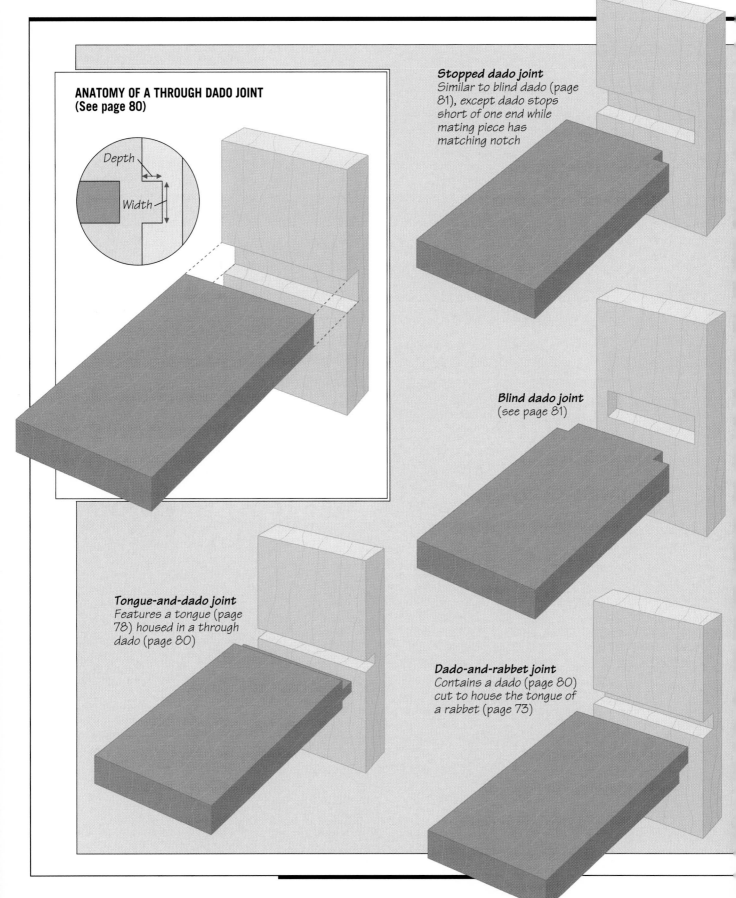

ANATOMY OF A THROUGH DADO JOINT
(See page 80)

Depth

Width

Stopped dado joint
Similar to blind dado (page 81), except dado stops short of one end while mating piece has matching notch

Blind dado joint
(see page 81)

Tongue-and-dado joint
Features a tongue (page 78) housed in a through dado (page 80)

Dado-and-rabbet joint
Contains a dado (page 80) cut to house the tongue of a rabbet (page 73)

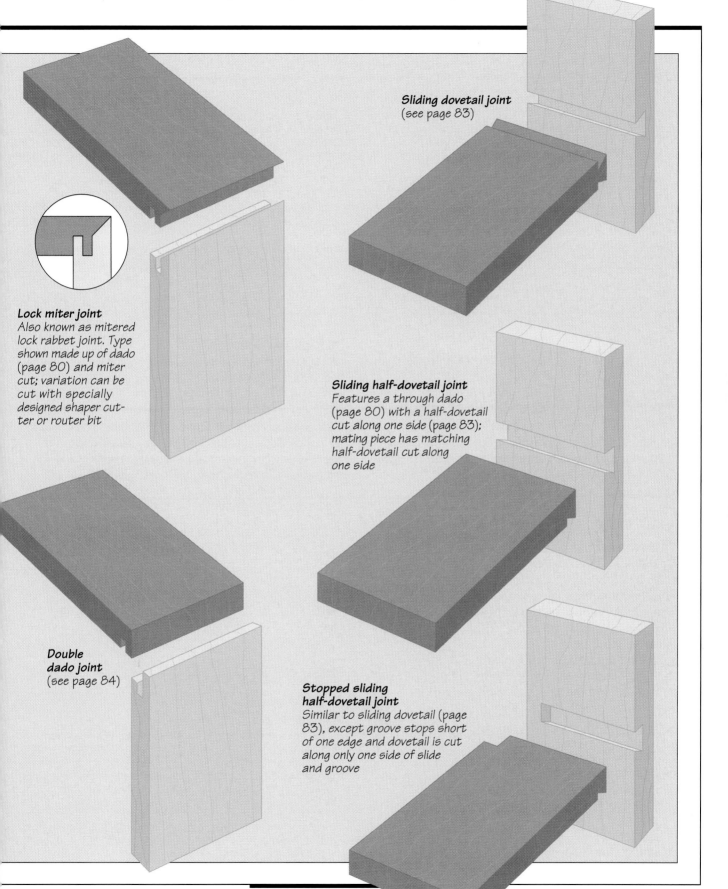

Sliding dovetail joint
(see page 83)

Lock miter joint
Also known as mitered lock rabbet joint. Type shown made up of dado (page 80) and miter cut; variation can be cut with specially designed shaper cutter or router bit

Sliding half-dovetail joint
Features a through dado (page 80) with a half-dovetail cut along one side (page 83); mating piece has matching half-dovetail cut along one side

Double dado joint
(see page 84)

Stopped sliding half-dovetail joint
Similar to sliding dovetail (page 83), except groove stops short of one edge and dovetail is cut along only one side of slide and groove

CORNER HALF-LAP JOINTS

The simple corner half-lap joint is frequently used to make frames. Adding dowels or screws to the joint provides an extra measure of strength.

MAKING A CORNER HALF-LAP JOINT

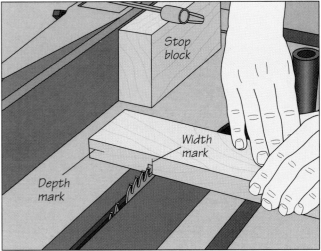

1 Cutting the shoulders
Make a half-lap on the table saw by cutting the shoulders first, and then the cheeks. Mark the depth and width of the half-lap on the edge of the workpiece, then install a crosscut blade and set the cutting height to one-half the stock thickness. Clamp a stop block to the rip fence; position the block so that the stock will clear it before reaching the blade. Align the width mark with the blade and position the fence for the width of cut. Then butt the end of the workpiece against the stop block and holding it in position on the miter gauge, feed it into the blade *(above)*.

2 Cutting the cheeks
Install a commercial tenoning jig on the table following the manufacturer's instructions; the model shown slides in the miter slot. (Instructions for building a shop-made tenoning jig are on page 93.) Clamp the workpiece to the jig, using a wood pad to protect the stock. Raise the blade to the width of the half-lap, then shift the jig laterally to line up the depth mark with the blade. Push the jig forward to make the cut *(right)*.

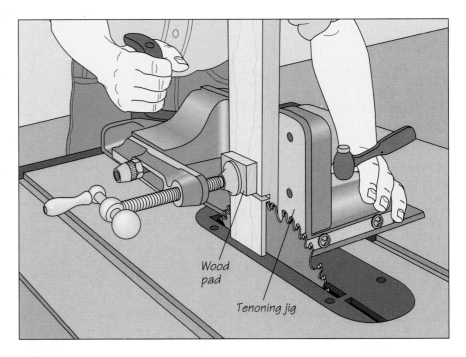

BUILD IT YOURSELF

CORNER HALF-LAP JOINT JIG

If you have to make corner half-laps in several boards of the same size, it is worth taking the time to build the jig at right. Cut the two base pieces and the stop block from plywood that is the same thickness as your stock. The base pieces should be wide enough to accommodate the edge guides and support the router base plate as you cut the half-laps. Use solid wood strips for the four edge guides.

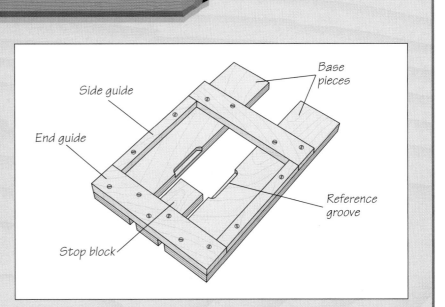

To assemble the jig, mark the shoulder of the half-lap on one workpiece and set the board face-up on a work surface. Butt the base pieces against the edges of the board so that the shoulder mark is near the middle of the base pieces. Install a straight bit in the router and align the cutter with the shoulder mark. Position one end guide across the base pieces and against the tool's base plate. Without moving the workpiece, repeat the procedure to position the opposite guide. Now align the bit with the edges of the workpiece and attach the side guides, leaving a slight gap between the router base plate and each guide. (The first half-lap you make with the jig will rout reference grooves in the base pieces.) Slip the stop block under the end guide, butt it against the end of the workpiece, and screw it in place. Countersink all fasteners.

To use the jig, clamp it to the work surface and slide the workpiece between the base pieces until it butts against the stop block. Protecting the stock with a wood pad, clamp the workpiece in place. Adjust the router's cutting depth to one-half

the stock thickness. Then, with the router positioned inside the guides, grip the tool firmly, turn it on and lower the bit into the workpiece. Guide the router in a clockwise direction to

cut the outside edges of the half-lap, keeping the base plate flush against a guide at all times. Then rout out the remaining waste, feeding the tool against the direction of bit rotation.

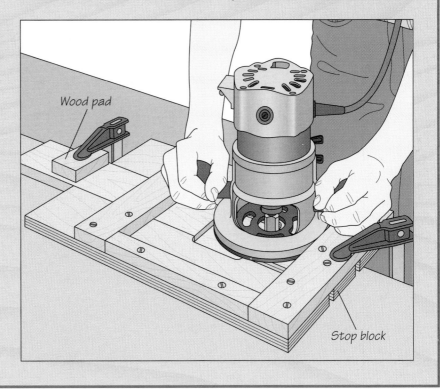

CROSS HALF-LAP JOINTS

Formed by cutting dadoes in two boards of equal thickness, the cross half-lap is an excellent method of joining the intersecting pieces of face frames. This joint requires no reinforcement.

ROUTING A CROSS HALF-LAP JOINT

Using a router and a shop-made jig

Build a jig like the one shown on page 65, but eliminate the stop block; this will allow you to align any section of the workpiece with the middle of the jig. Make a test cut in a scrap board to rout reference grooves in the base pieces. These will make it easy to line up the cuts. Mark shoulder lines for the half-laps on the workpieces, then install a straight bit in the router and set the cutting depth for half the thickness of the stock. Position the stock in the jig, aligning the shoulder marks with the reference grooves in the base pieces. Clamp the jig to the work surface, then install a second clamp to secure the workpiece in place. Rout the half-lap *(right)* as you would to make a corner half-lap joint.

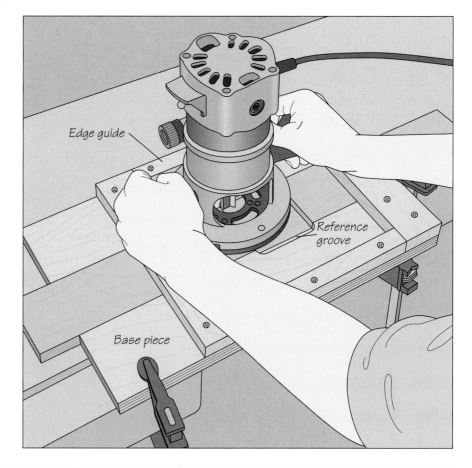

Edge guide

Reference groove

Base piece

HALF-BLIND HALF-LAP JOINTS

A variation of the T half-lap, the half-blind half-lap joint conceals the end grain of one member. The socket for the half-lap can be cut with a router, as shown below, or by hand using a chisel.

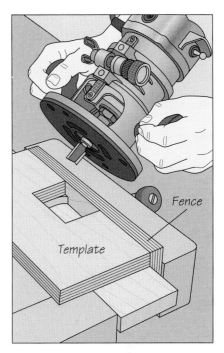

MAKING A HALF-BLIND HALF-LAP JOINT

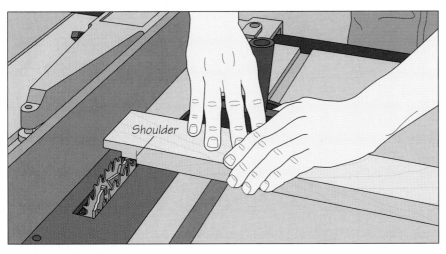

1 Cutting the half-lap
Make this joint by cutting the half-lap on the table saw first, and then routing out the socket. Mark the shoulder of the half-lap on the leading edge of one piece. Install a dado head and set the cutting height to one-half the stock thickness. Butt the shoulder mark against the outside blade of the dado head, then position the rip fence flush against the workpiece. Cut away the waste in successive passes, working from the end of the board to the shoulder mark. Make the final pass with the board flush against the fence *(above)*. **(Caution: Blade guard removed for clarity.)**

2 Cutting the joint socket
A plywood template is used to rout out the socket. Outline the half-lap cut in Step 1 on the template, then cut out the pattern with a band saw, saber saw or coping saw. Fasten a fence to the cut-out edge of the template with countersunk screws. Secure the template and the workpiece in a vise, aligning the cut-out with the outline on the stock. Install a top-piloted straight bit in your router and make the cutting depth equal to one-half the stock thickness plus the thickness of the template. Rout the outline of the socket by keeping the bit pilot against the template, then remove the remaining waste by moving the router in a clockwise direction, against the direction of bit rotation. Use a chisel to square the corners.

ANGLED HALF-LAP JOINTS

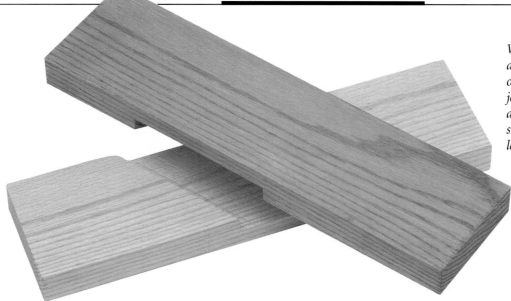

Woodworkers use the angled half-lap—or oblique lap joint—to join boards that cross at angles other than 90°, such as diagonal table leg stretchers.

CUTTING AN ANGLED HALF-LAP JOINT

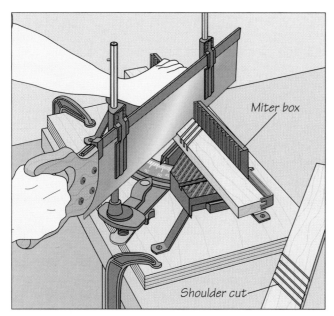

Miter box

Shoulder cut

1 Cutting kerfs in the half-lap outline
Mark the shoulders of the half-lap on the face of the workpiece, angling the lines to suit the job at hand. The cuts can be made with a radial arm saw, table saw, router, or, as shown here, a handsaw and miter box. Set the workpiece in the miter box with the edge against the fence and align one shoulder mark with the blade. Lock the blade at this angle and adjust the depth to one-half the stock thickness. Hold the board in position as you saw into it. Repeat to cut the other shoulder line. Then saw a number of kerfs between the two cuts *(above)*.

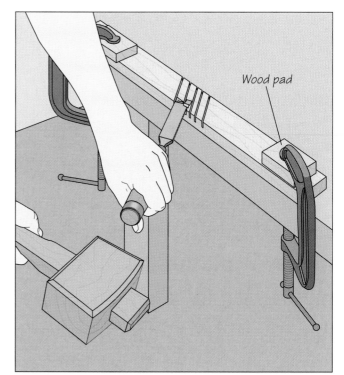

Wood pad

2 Chiseling out the waste
Clamp the workpiece face-up on the bench, protecting the stock with wood pads. Holding a wood chisel bevel-up horizontally, strike the handle with a mallet to split off the waste between the shoulder cuts *(above)*. After the bulk of the waste has been removed, pare the bottom of the half-lap until it is smooth and even.

DOVETAILED HALF-LAP JOINTS

Combining the strength of the dovetail joint with the simplicity of the half-lap, the dovetailed half-lap is a favorite joinery method for frames and table stretchers. The joint strongly resists tension.

MAKING A DOVETAILED HALF-LAP JOINT

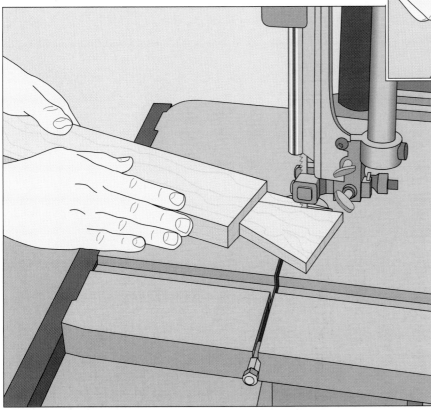

Shoulder

Cutting the dovetailed half-lap and the socket

In one workpiece, cut a corner half-lap *(page 64)*. Then, outline the dovetail on the cheek of the half-lap and cut it out on the band saw *(left)*; use an angle of 1:8 if you are working with hardwood, or a 1:6 angle for softwood. Use the dovetailed half-lap to outline the socket in the mating workpiece; make sure the shoulder of the half-lap is butted against the edge of the board as you mark the lines *(above)*. Make the socket using a router with a template *(page 67)*, a table saw, a radial arm saw, or a handsaw and miter box *(page 68)*, cutting to one-half the stock thickness.

GLAZING BAR HALF-LAP JOINTS

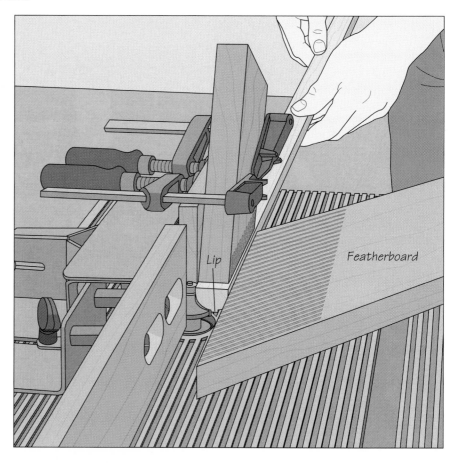

For many of us, the glazing, or sash, bar half-lap joint is as familiar as the view from the kitchen window. Featuring a mitered half-lap cut into a molded wood strip, the joint has traditionally been used to create a grid to hold the glass panes of a cabinet door or window. The panes sit in rabbets routed along the edges of the bars and are held in place with thin strips of molding.

MAKING A GLAZING BAR HALF-LAP JOINT

1 Molding the glazing bar
This joint is made in three stages: First, the proper profile is cut into the glazing bar, as shown at right; next, rabbets are cut into the opposite side of the bar to hold the glass and molding strips *(step 2)*; finally, the mitered half-lap is produced *(steps 3 to 5)*. For the first stage, install a piloted round-over bit in a router, mount the tool in a table, and align the fence with the bit's pilot bearing. The stock should be wide enough so that making a pass on each side of the bar will leave a ¼-inch-wide lip between the cuts. Support the workpiece during the operation with three featherboards: Clamp one to the table opposite the bit and two to the fence on either side of the cutter. (In the illustration, the featherboard on the outfeed side of the fence has been removed for clarity.) Feed the bar into the bit until your fingers approach the bit, then use the next piece as a push stick or move to the other side of the table and pull the workpiece past the cutter. Repeat the cut on the other side of the bar *(right)*. Prepare an extra bar to help set up the cut in step 3.

Lip

Featherboard

2 Cutting rabbets for the glass panes

Install a dado head on your table saw slightly wider than the desired rabbets. The tongue remaining after the rabbets are cut should measure at least ¼ inch. Install a wooden auxiliary fence and mark the rabbet depth on it—the combined thickness of the glass and the molding strip. Position the auxiliary fence over the dado head, ensuring that the metal fence is clear of the cutters. Turn on the saw and slowly crank up the dado head until it forms a relief cut to the marked line. Turn off the saw and mark the width of the rabbets on the leading end of the glazing bar. Butt one of the marks against the outer blade of the dado head, then position the fence flush against the bar. Use three featherboards to support the workpiece as in step 1, adding a support board to provide extra pressure for the featherboard clamped to the table. (Again in this illustration, one of the featherboards has been removed for clarity.) Feed the bars by hand *(right)* until your fingers approach the featherboards, then use the next workpiece to push the bar through. Finish the cuts on the final workpiece by pulling it from the outfeed side of the table.

Auxiliary fence

Relief cut

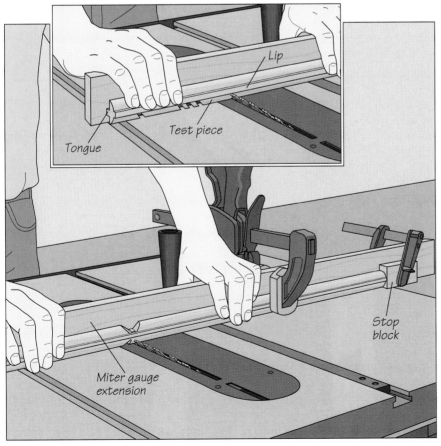

Lip

Test piece

Tongue

Miter gauge extension

Stop block

3 Making the miter cuts

Remove the dado head and install a crosscut blade. Adjust the blade angle to 45°, then attach a miter gauge extension. To set the blade height, hold the extra glazing bar on the saw table so the tongue you cut in step 2 is flush against the extension. The top of the blade should be level with the lower side of the lip. Make a test cut and adjust the blade height until the cutting edge just scores the lip *(inset)*. Then mark out the miter cuts on both sides of the bars; at their widest point the Vs should be the same width as the stock. To make the cut, hold the tongue of the bar flat against the miter gauge extension and align one of the marks with the blade. Butt a stop block against the end of the stock and clamp it to the extension to line up subsequent cuts. Clamp the workpiece to the extension and feed the glazing bar into the blade while holding it firmly in place. Rotate the piece and repeat to cut the other side of the V. Repeat the process to cut the V on the opposite side of the bar *(left)*.

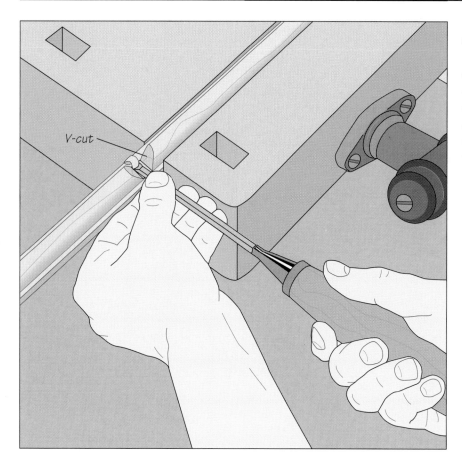

4 Cleaning up the V-cuts
Once all the miter cuts have been made, use a narrow chisel to pare away the waste. The width of the channel at the bottom of the V should equal the width of the lip. Holding the chisel bevel side up, pare away the waste *(left)* until the bottom of the V is smooth and flat. Work carefully to avoid tearout.

5 Cutting the half-laps
Adjust the table saw dado head to the width of the bar's lip and set the cutting height to one-half the stock thickness. You will be cutting a half-lap in the bottom of one glazing bar, then making an identical cut in the top of the mating piece. Set up the cut by aligning the middle of the V-cut with the dado head, while holding the bar flush against the miter gauge extension. Keep the workpiece flat on the saw table and flush against the extension as you cut the half-laps *(below)*.

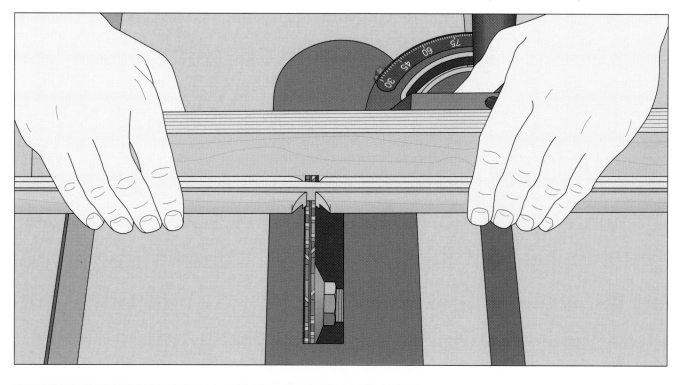

RABBET JOINTS

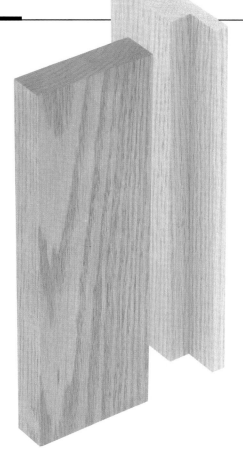

Widely used in carcase and drawer construction, the rabbet joint is essentially a modified butt joint in which the end or edge of one board fits in a rabbet cut in the mating piece. The rabbet's width should equal the thickness of the stock; its depth should be half that amount.

MAKING A RABBET JOINT

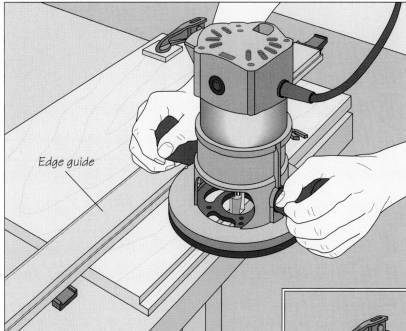

Edge guide

Using a router
You can use either a piloted bit or a non-piloted bit with an edge guide. In either case, clamp the stock to a work surface. For a non-piloted bit, mark the rabbet width on the top face of the stock. Align the cutting edge of the bit with the mark, then clamp an edge guide to the workpiece flush against the router base plate and parallel to the workpiece edge. Cut the rabbet with the plate butted against the guide *(above)*. If you are working with a piloted bit, choose a cutter that will produce the desired width of rabbet. Then, gripping the router firmly with both hands, guide the bit into the workpiece at one end. Ride the pilot bearing along the edge *(right)* as you make the cut.

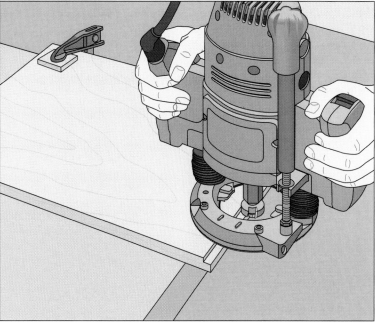

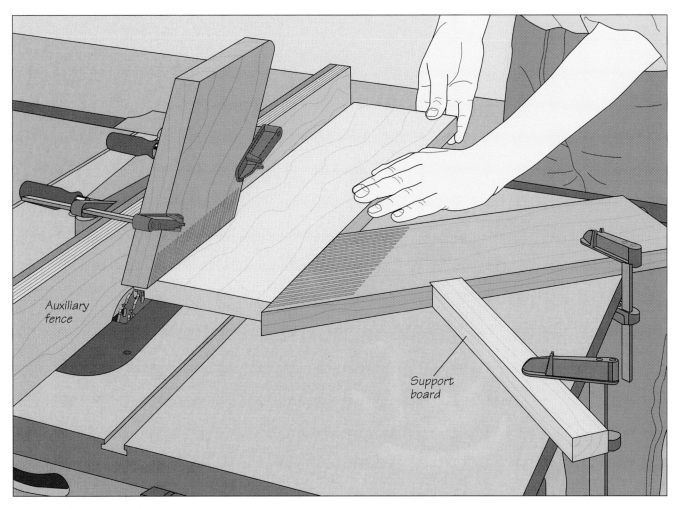

Auxiliary
fence

Support
board

Cutting a rabbet on the table saw
Install a dado head slightly wider than the rabbet you wish to make, then install an auxiliary fence and make a relief cut in it as you would when cutting a glazing bar half-lap *(page 71)*. Mark a cutting line for the inside edge of the rabbet on the workpiece. Butt the mark against the outer blade of the dado head, then position the rip fence flush against the workpiece. Clamp two featherboards to hold the workpiece securely against the fence and saw table; a support board provides extra stability. Feed the workpiece with both hands *(above)* until the rabbet is completed. Use a push stick to finish the pass on narrow stock.

SHOP TIP

Minimizing tearout
Router bits can tear wood fibers as they exit a workpiece at the end of a crossgrain rabbet or dado cut. To prevent splintering, clamp a wood block the same thickness as your workpiece along the edge from which the bit will exit. The pressure of the block against the stock will compress the fibers and reduce the problem of tearout.

STOPPED RABBET JOINTS

The stopped rabbet joint is similar to the standard rabbet, with an important difference: The rabbet cut is stopped short of the front edge of the joint—usually by no more than 1 inch—and a matching notch is cut in the mating piece, resulting in an invisible joint.

TWO WAYS TO ROUT A STOPPED RABBET

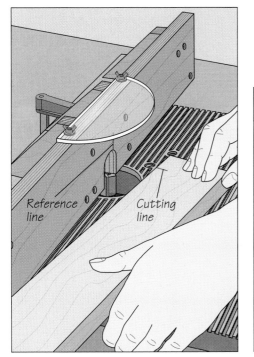

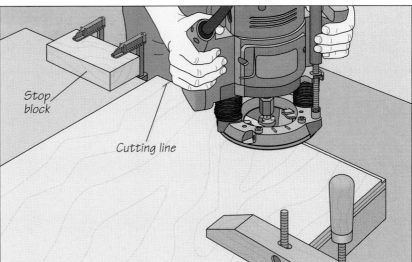

Routing a stopped rabbet

Make the cut on a router table or with the router hand-held. In either case, mark a cutting line on the face of the workpiece for the end of the rabbet. For the router-table method, install a straight bit, set the depth of cut, and adjust the fence for the desired width of cut. Draw a reference line on the fence to mark the position of the cutter where it exits the fence. With the stock clear of the bit, turn on the router and press the workpiece flush against the fence while feeding it forward. When the cutting line on the board lines up with the reference line, pivot the stock off the fence *(above, left)*. To make the cut with a hand-held router, install a piloted rabbeting bit and clamp the stock to a work surface. Align the bit with the cutting line on the workpiece and clamp a stop block against the router base plate. Feed the bit into the stock at the starting end of the rabbet, butting the bit's pilot bearing against the edge. Continue the cut along the edge *(above, right)* until the base plate touches the stop block. For both methods, square the end of the rabbet with a chisel.

MITERED RABBET JOINTS

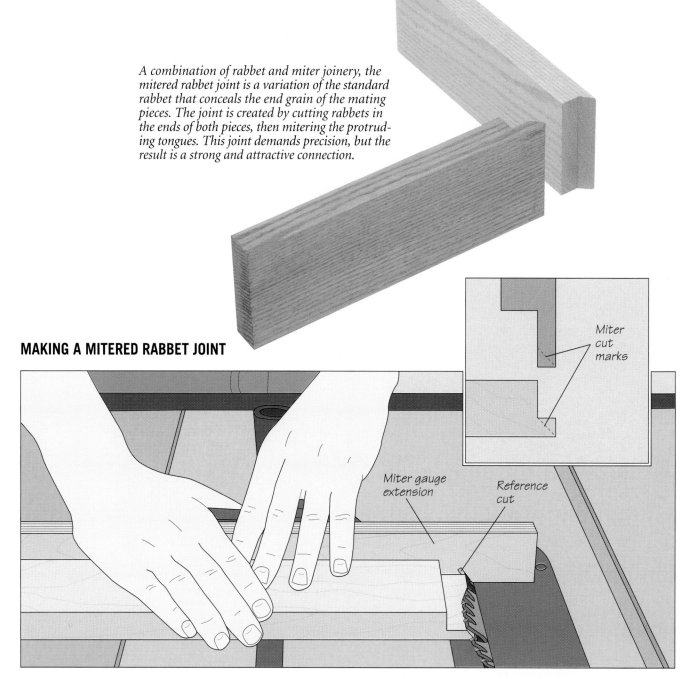

A combination of rabbet and miter joinery, the mitered rabbet joint is a variation of the standard rabbet that conceals the end grain of the mating pieces. The joint is created by cutting rabbets in the ends of both pieces, then mitering the protruding tongues. This joint demands precision, but the result is a strong and attractive connection.

MAKING A MITERED RABBET JOINT

Miter cut marks

Miter gauge extension

Reference cut

Cutting the rabbets and miters

Cut rabbets in both pieces. Make the cuts to the same depth—about two-thirds the thickness of the stock. The width of one rabbet should equal the stock's thickness, the width of the other should equal the thickness of the tongue left by the first rabbet cut. Mark 45° angle lines across both tongues for the miter cuts, starting each mark at the outside corner of the tongue *(inset)*. Adjust the blade angle on your table saw to 45°, and set the cut-

ting height so the blade will cut through the tongue. Next, screw an extension board to the miter gauge and make a reference cut in the board. Holding the workpiece flush against the extension, align the cutting line with the reference cut, then cut the miter *(above)*. When mitering the workpiece with the shorter tongue, adjust the cutting height to just sever the waste; otherwise, the blade will bite into the rabbet shoulder and weaken the joint.

TONGUE-AND-GROOVE JOINTS

The tongue-and-groove joint has many uses for the woodworker—from joining boards edge-to-edge to fixing shelving to carcases. When used to form carcase panels, the joint can be assembled without glue to allow for wood movement caused by fluctuations in humidity.

A TONGUE-AND-GROOVE JOINT ON THE TABLE SAW

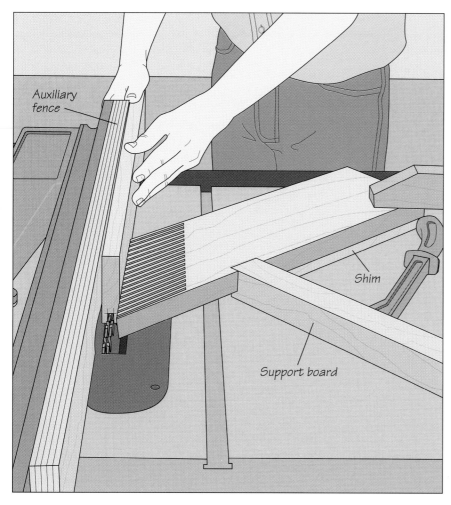

Auxiliary fence

Shim

Support board

1 Cutting the groove
Mark the outline of the groove on the end of the workpiece. It should be ⅓ the stock thickness; the depth is often ½ inch. Install a dado head and adjust it to the desired width and height. Install an auxiliary wood fence and make a relief cut in it *(page 71)*. (Although the auxiliary fence is only necessary for cutting the tongue in step 2, it is better to mount it now.) Align the cutting marks with the dado head, butt the rip fence against the stock, and clamp a featherboard to the table for support. Rest the featherboard on a wood shim to keep the workpiece from tipping and clamp a support board against the featherboard for extra pressure. Press the workpiece against the fence as you feed the stock into the dado head *(left)*. Complete the pass with a push stick.

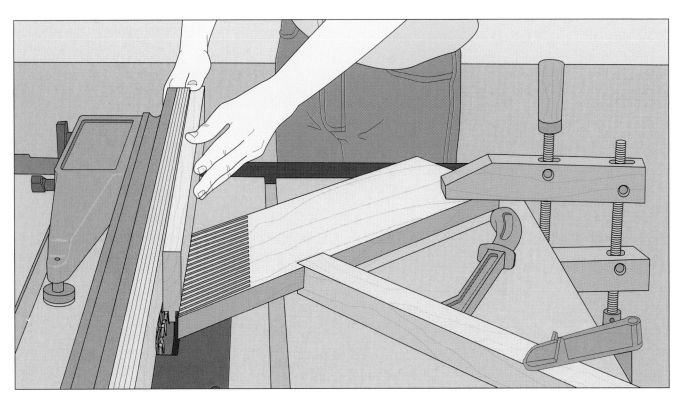

2 Cutting the tongue

Mark the tongue on the leading end of the workpiece, using the groove from step 1 as a guide. Adjust the dado head for a slightly wider cut and lower the cutting height a little so the tongue will not reach the bottom of the groove. Align the dado head with one of the cutting marks and move the fence against the stock; also position the featherboard and support board. Feed the board as you did cutting the groove, using a push stick to complete the pass. Turn the workpiece end-for-end and repeat on the other side of the tongue *(above)*. Test-fit the tongue in the groove and adjust the rip fence, if necessary.

SHOP TIP

Rabbeting on the jointer
If your jointer has a rabbeting ledge, it can cut rabbets along either the face or edge of a board. In fact, many woodworkers consider the jointer the best tool for rabbeting with the grain of a workpiece. Adjust the cutting depth to no more than 1/8 inch, then align your cutting mark for the rabbet with the end of the jointer knives and butt the fence against the stock. Keep the workpiece flat on the table and butted against the fence as you make the pass. For a rabbet along a board face, use a push block. Make as many passes as necessary, increasing the cutting depth 1/8 inch at a time.

GLUE JOINTS

The glue joint is a variation of the standard tongue-and-groove and is easily produced with the router or the shaper.

MAKING A GLUE JOINT ON THE ROUTER TABLE

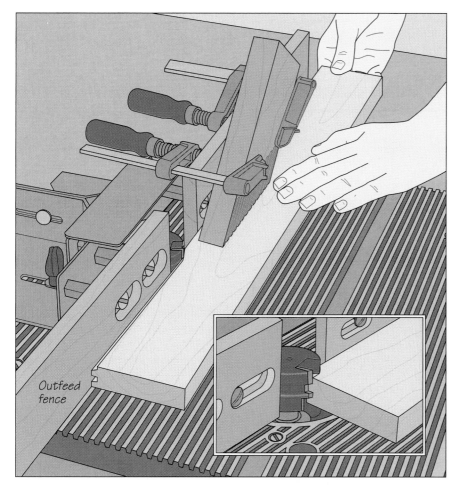

Outfeed fence

Making the cuts

Install a glue joint bit in a router and mount the tool in a table. Adjust the cutting depth so that the thickness of the waste removed by the upper part of the cutter will equal the thickness of the stock left below the bottom part of the cutter *(inset)*. Position the fence so that the bit makes a full cut in the board, removing the entire edge. Secure the workpiece with two featherboards clamped to the fence on both sides of the bit; in the illustration, the featherboard on the outfeed side has been removed for clarity. To make a pass, feed the stock into the bit with your right hand while pressing it firmly against the fence with your left hand. To keep the entire edge flush against the fence throughout the operation, adjust the outfeed part of the fence when the board reaches it. Stop the cut and turn off the machine, but do not remove the workpiece. Holding the workpiece in place, advance the outfeed fence until it butts against the cut edge. Then complete the pass *(left)*.

THROUGH DADO JOINTS

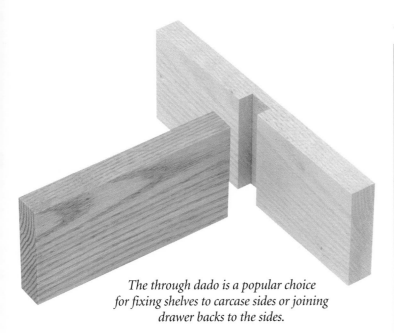

The through dado is a popular choice for fixing shelves to carcase sides or joining drawer backs to the sides.

A THROUGH DADO ON THE RADIAL ARM SAW

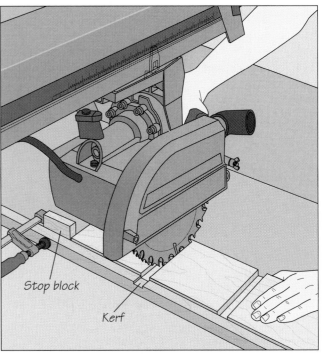

Stop block

Kerf

Cutting repeat dadoes

Install a dado head and adjust it to the desired width of the dado. Set the saw in the 90° crosscutting position and adjust the cutting depth to cut a dado halfway through the workpiece. Cut a kerf through the fence, then mark cutting lines for the width of the dadoes on the workpiece. Push the saw yoke and dado head behind the fence and align one set of cutting marks on the workpiece with the kerf in the fence. Then, holding the workpiece snugly against the fence, make the cut. Slide the workpiece to the next set of cutting lines and cut the next dado the same way. To help line up repeat cuts, clamp a stop block to the fence (above).

SHOP TIP

A jig for equally spaced dadoes
You can cut precisely spaced dadoes on your table saw quickly and accurately by using a miter gauge extension and a wooden key. After your dado head is installed and adjusted to the proper width, cut two appropriately spaced dadoes in a miter gauge extension board. Screw the extension to the gauge, carefully aligning one dado with the dado head and offsetting the second cut to the right; insert a wooden key into this dado. Cut the first dado in your workpiece. To achieve proper spacing for the second cut, slide your workpiece to the right and place the first dado over the key. Make the second dado cut and repeat the process until the job is completed.

BLIND DADO JOINTS

The blind dado joint, in which the dado stops short of both edges of the board, is just as strong as the through dado, but invisible once it is assembled. The joint is commonly used for attaching shelving to cabinets.

ROUTING A BLIND DADO

Stop block

Edge guide

Using a plunge router

Set the stock on a work surface and mark out the dado; it should be as wide as the thickness of the mating board. Install a straight bit the same width as the dado. Align the bit over the width marks for the cut and clamp an edge guide to the workpiece flush against the router base plate. Then line up the bit with each of the dado end marks and clamp stop blocks to the workpiece. Gripping the router firmly with both hands, butt its base plate against the edge guide and one stop block and plunge the bit into the stock. Cut along the guide *(left)* until the base plate touches the other stop block. You will need to square the ends of the dado with a chisel and cut notches at both edges of the mating board to fit it into the dado.

BUILD IT YOURSELF

ADJUSTABLE DADO JIG

The jig at right will enable you to rout dadoes quickly and accurately. With its adjustable fence, it can also help solve the problem of making dadoes that are wider than the diameter of your largest straight bit. Cut the parts of the jig from either plywood or solid wood; the dimensions shown in the illustration will suit most routers.

Attach the base pieces to the cleats so their outer edges are flush. Fasten the fixed fence in place flush with the outside edge of the narrower base piece, countersinking all the screws. To attach the adjustable fence, bore holes through the cleats at each end of the wider base piece for a hanger bolt. Screw the bolts to the jig, leaving about 1 inch of each one protruding above the base piece. To prepare the adjustable fence, cut a 1-inch-long slot at each end. Make the slots slightly wider than the bolts, ensuring that they will line up with the bolts when the fence is installed. (You can make the slots by boring a row of connected holes on the drill press and cleaning up the cuts with a chisel.) Use washers and wing nuts to attach the adjustable fence to the wider base piece.

To use the jig, set your stock on a work surface and outline the dado on it. Align the edge of the narrower base piece with one edge of the outline and clamp the jig to the work surface. Place the router on the base pieces, butting its base plate against the fixed fence. Loosen the wing nuts and slide the adjustable fence against the base plate. Tighten the nuts, check that the fences are parallel,

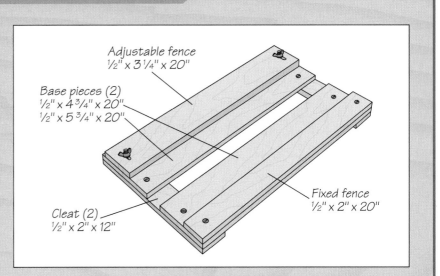

Adjustable fence
1/2" x 3 1/4" x 20"

Base pieces (2)
1/2" x 4 3/4" x 20"
1/2" x 5 3/4" x 20"

Fixed fence
1/2" x 2" x 20"

Cleat (2)
1/2" x 2" x 12"

and rout the dado, riding the base plate along the fences throughout the cut *(below)*. For a dado that is wider than your bit's diameter, slide the adjustable fence away from the base plate by the appropriate amount, measuring to make sure the distance between fences is uniform along their length. Ride the base plate against the fences to rout the edges of the dado, then remove the waste between the cuts.

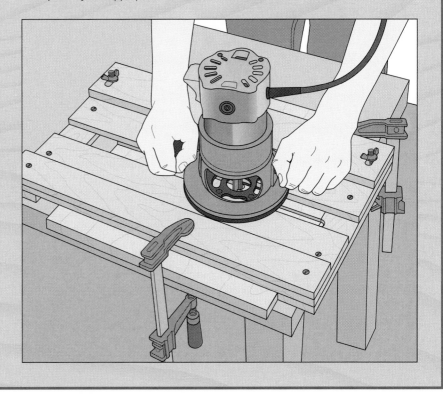

SLIDING DOVETAIL JOINTS

The sliding dovetail is commonly used to assemble drawers, attach crown molding to cabinets, and install shelves in carcases. Because glue is not required to lock the mating pieces together, the joint is a good choice for furniture that must be disassembled.

A SLIDING DOVETAIL JOINT ON THE ROUTER TABLE

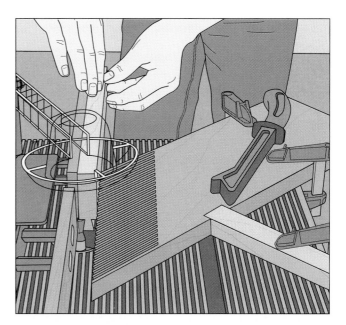

Featherboard

Push stick

1 Routing the dovetail groove

Cut the groove in two passes, first with a straight bit to remove most of the waste, and then with a dovetail bit to complete the groove. For the first pass, install a ¼-inch straight bit in the router and mount the tool in a table. Set the cutting depth, then center an edge of the workpiece over the bit and butt the fence against its face. To keep the workpiece flush against the fence, clamp a featherboard to the table. Complete the pass with a push stick. Install a dovetail bit in the router and make the second pass the same way *(above)*.

2 Making the dovetail slide

With the dovetail bit still in the router, reduce the cutting depth slightly. This will make the slide shorter than the depth of the groove, improving the fit of the joint. Move the fence toward the bit until about half the diameter of the cutter projects beyond the fence; reposition the featherboard accordingly. Cut the slide in two passes: Make the first pass the same way you routed the groove, pressing the face of the stock flush against the fence. To complete the slide, turn the workpiece end-for-end and make the second pass with the opposite face of the stock running along the fence *(above)*. Test-fit the slide in the groove, then move the fence away from the bit for subsequent cuts, until the slide fits.

DOUBLE DADO JOINTS

The double dado joint mates two through dadoes—one on a face and the other, with one tongue shortened, on an end. The joint is stronger than an ordinary through dado because it provides more gluing surface. It works well when pieces of different thicknesses must be joined together, making it ideal for joining a drawer front to the sides.

A DOUBLE DADO JOINT ON THE TABLE SAW

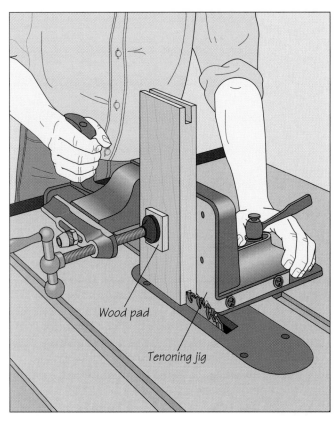

Wood pad

Tenoning jig

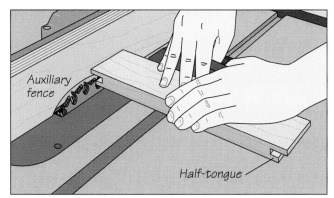

Auxiliary fence

Half-tongue

1 Making the cuts

Install a dado head on your saw, adjusting its width to one-third the stock thickness. Also install a tenoning jig; the commercial model shown slides in the miter slot. Clamp the workpiece to the jig, protecting the stock with a wood pad. Adjust the jig to center the edge of the workpiece on the blades so that the dado will be cut in the middle third of the board. Slide the jig forward to feed the stock, then turn the workpiece end-for-end and repeat to cut the dado in the other end *(left)*. Next, install an auxiliary fence and notch it *(page 71)*. Mark a cutting line on one of the tongues on the inside face of the board to divide it in half. Holding the workpiece flush against the miter gauge, inside-face down, align the mark with the dado head. Butt the fence against the stock and adjust the cutting height to cut the tongue in half. Feed the workpiece with the miter gauge to make the cut; repeat on the other end *(above)*. Complete the joint by cutting matching dadoes in the face of the mating pieces to accept the half-tongues.

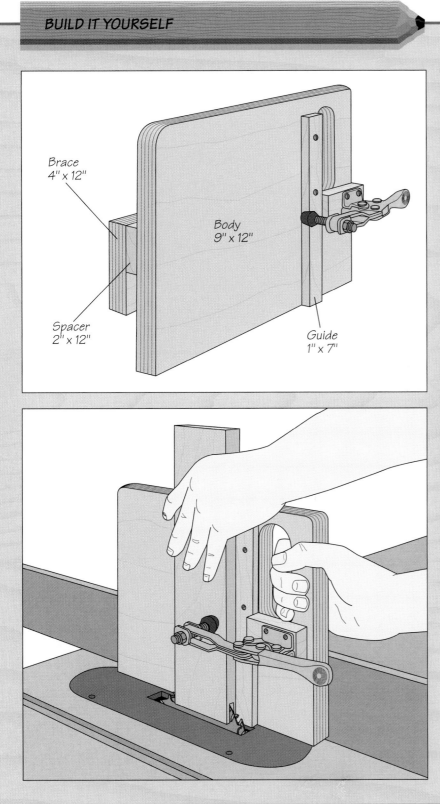

Brace
4" x 12"

Body
9" x 12"

Spacer
2" x 12"

Guide
1" x 7"

TABLE-SAW END-DADOING JIG

Easy to assemble, the fence-straddling jig shown at left works well for cutting dadoes in the ends of boards. (The jig can also be used to cut half-lap joints or two-shouldered open mortise-and-tenon joints.) Refer to the dimensions suggested in the illustration, making sure the thickness of the spacer and width of the brace allow the jig to slide smoothly along your rip fence without wobbling.

Cut the body and brace from ³/₄-inch plywood and the guide and spacer from solid wood. Saw an oval hole for a handle in one corner of the jig body. Attach the guide to the body directly in front of the handle hole, making sure that it is perfectly vertical. (The screws should be in the top half of the guide, because the blade will cut into it for some cuts.) Screw a small wood block to the body below the hole and attach a toggle clamp to the block. Finally, fasten the spacer and brace in place.

To use the jig, place it astride the fence. Butt the workpiece against the jig guide and clamp it in place. Position the fence to align the cutting marks on the board with the blade and slide the jig along the fence to make the cut (left, bottom).

MORTISE-AND-TENON JOINTS

The mortise-and-tenon joint is one of the oldest methods of fastening wood. It was relied upon by builders of the sarcophagi of ancient Egypt and, centuries later, the sailing ships of Columbus. Today, the joint is used most often in furnituremaking—most typically for building frames in frame-and-panel construction and joining rails to legs on desks, tables, and chairs.

The joint consists of two key elements: the tenon, a projection from the end of one board that fits into a slot—the mortise—in the mating piece. The mortise-and-tenon features a relatively large gluing area, involving good contact between long-grain surfaces—the cheeks of the tenon and the sides of the mortise. Provided the tenon fits snugly in the mortise, the joint offers virtually unparalleled resistance to most of the stresses that wood joints endure. Only the dovetail joint is more difficult to pull apart.

There are dozens of variations of the standard joint, and many are shown in the inventory of joints on pages 88 and 89. For example, the tusk tenon is a common way of reinforcing a trestle table; a variation of the round tenon serves both an

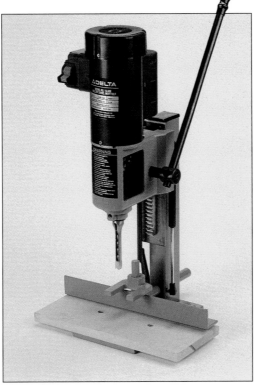

The hollow chisel mortiser can drill mortises up to 3 inches deep quickly and accurately. The bench-mounted tool is fitted with the same chisel bits and mortising attachment used by the drill press.

esthetic and a structural role in Windsor chairs.

Whether a tenon is haunched, wedged, pegged, rounded, or angled, a few rules of thumb dictate the proportions when cutting this joint. The thickness of a tenon should be one-third the thickness of the workpiece; its width may be from two-thirds of the width to the full width of the workpiece.

A tenon's length depends on whether it passes completely through the mortise workpiece or remains hidden, or blind. The length of a blind tenon *(page 94)* is often ¾ inch or longer, depending on the use of the mating workpiece; a through tenon *(page 97)* will be as long as the width or thickness of the mortise workpiece.

The pages that follow show several hand- and power-tool methods for cutting mortise-and-tenon joints. Tenons can be cut on the table saw *(page 92)*, with a backsaw *(page 95)*, or on the drill press *(page 110)*. Mortises can be produced on the table saw or drill press, chiseled out by hand *(page 94)*, or routed *(page 97)*. Choose the method that suits your needs and the tools in your shop.

A tenon at the end of a rail fits snugly in a mortise cut out of a table leg. This blind mortise-and-tenon joint is both sturdy and long-lasting.

MORTISE-AND-TENON JOINTS AND JIGS

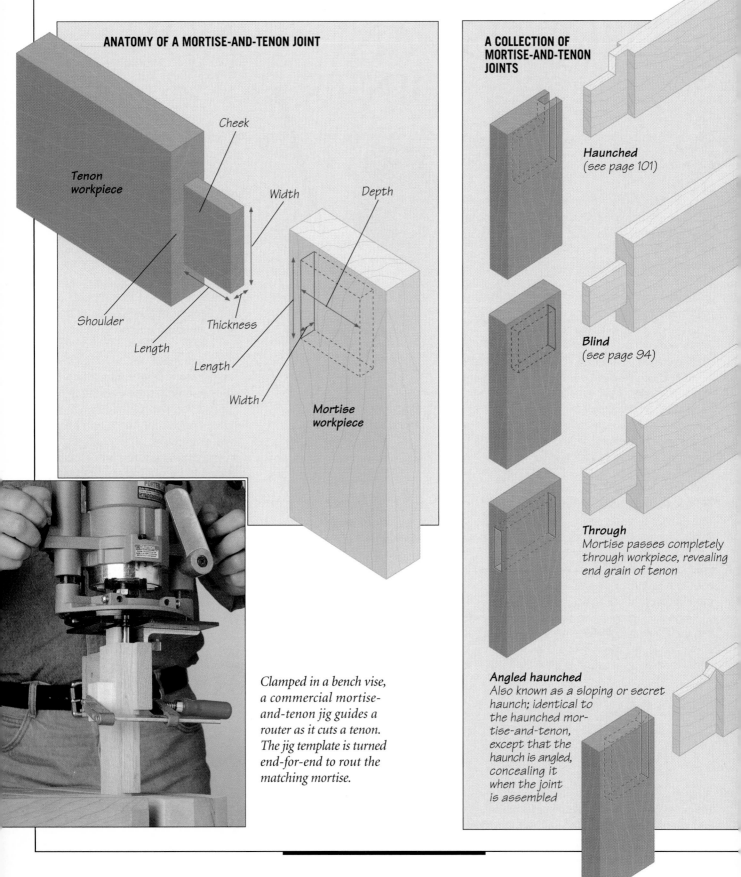

ANATOMY OF A MORTISE-AND-TENON JOINT

Tenon workpiece

Cheek

Width

Depth

Shoulder

Length

Thickness

Length

Width

Mortise workpiece

Clamped in a bench vise, a commercial mortise-and-tenon jig guides a router as it cuts a tenon. The jig template is turned end-for-end to rout the matching mortise.

A COLLECTION OF MORTISE-AND-TENON JOINTS

Haunched
(see page 101)

Blind
(see page 94)

Through
Mortise passes completely through workpiece, revealing end grain of tenon

Angled haunched
Also known as a sloping or secret haunch; identical to the haunched mortise-and-tenon, except that the haunch is angled, concealing it when the joint is assembled

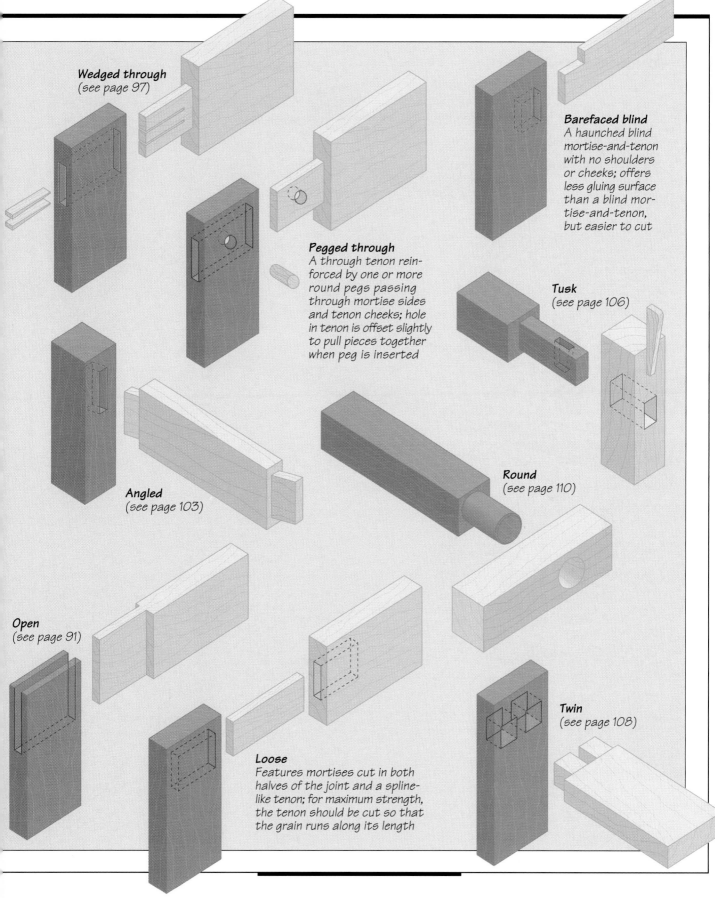

Wedged through
(see page 97)

Barefaced blind
A haunched blind mortise-and-tenon with no shoulders or cheeks; offers less gluing surface than a blind mortise-and-tenon, but easier to cut

Pegged through
A through tenon reinforced by one or more round pegs passing through mortise sides and tenon cheeks; hole in tenon is offset slightly to pull pieces together when peg is inserted

Tusk
(see page 106)

Angled
(see page 103)

Round
(see page 110)

Open
(see page 91)

Twin
(see page 108)

Loose
Features mortises cut in both halves of the joint and a spline-like tenon; for maximum strength, the tenon should be cut so that the grain runs along its length

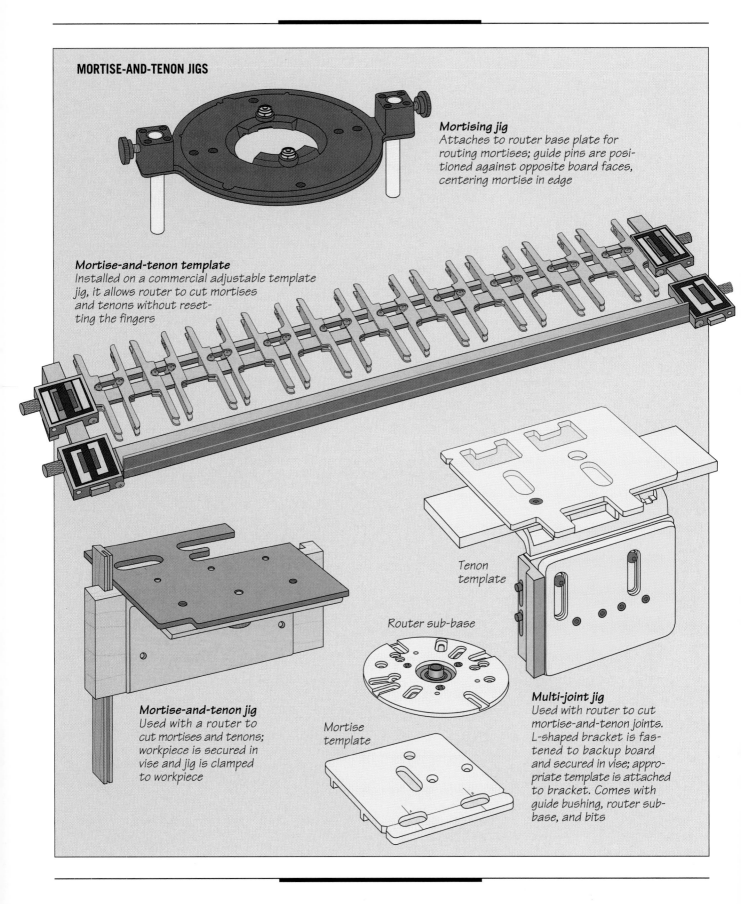

MORTISE-AND-TENON JIGS

Mortising jig
Attaches to router base plate for routing mortises; guide pins are positioned against opposite board faces, centering mortise in edge

Mortise-and-tenon template
Installed on a commercial adjustable template jig, it allows router to cut mortises and tenons without resetting the fingers

Tenon template

Router sub-base

Mortise-and-tenon jig
Used with a router to cut mortises and tenons; workpiece is secured in vise and jig is clamped to workpiece

Mortise template

Multi-joint jig
Used with router to cut mortise-and-tenon joints. L-shaped bracket is fastened to backup board and secured in vise; appropriate template is attached to bracket. Comes with guide bushing, router sub-base, and bits

OPEN MORTISE-AND-TENON JOINTS

Also known as a bridle joint or slip joint, the open mortise-and-tenon is commonly used in frame construction. Both the open mortise and two-shouldered tenon can be cut on a table saw or radial arm saw.

AN OPEN MORTISE-AND-TENON ON THE TABLE SAW

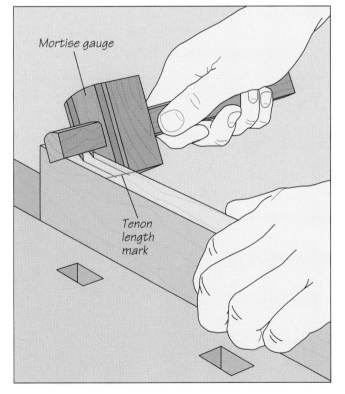

Mortise gauge

Tenon length mark

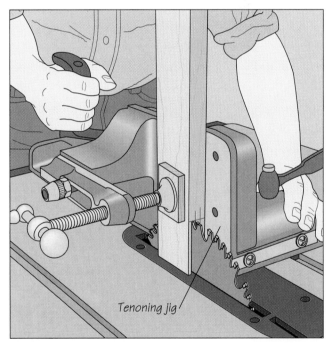

Tenoning jig

1 Outlining the tenon

Secure the stock edge-up in a vise and mark a line across the edge for the tenon length. Then adjust a mortise gauge so that the gap between its pins equals the tenon thickness—typically one-third the thickness of the workpiece. Adjust the mortise gauge so that the tenon outline is centered between opposing faces of the workpiece. Hold the stock flush against the face of the workpiece as you guide the gauge along the surface, scribing the sides of the tenon outline in the wood *(above)*.

2 Cutting the tenon cheeks

Make a tenon with the table saw by cutting the cheeks first, and then the shoulders. Install a tenoning jig on the table; the model shown slides in the miter slot. Protecting the stock with a wood pad, clamp the workpiece to the jig and raise the blade to the tenon length mark. Position the jig so that one of the cutting lines for the sides of the tenon is aligned with the blade. Feed the jig forward to make the cut *(above)*. Turn off the saw, turn the workpiece around in the jig, and cut the other cheek.

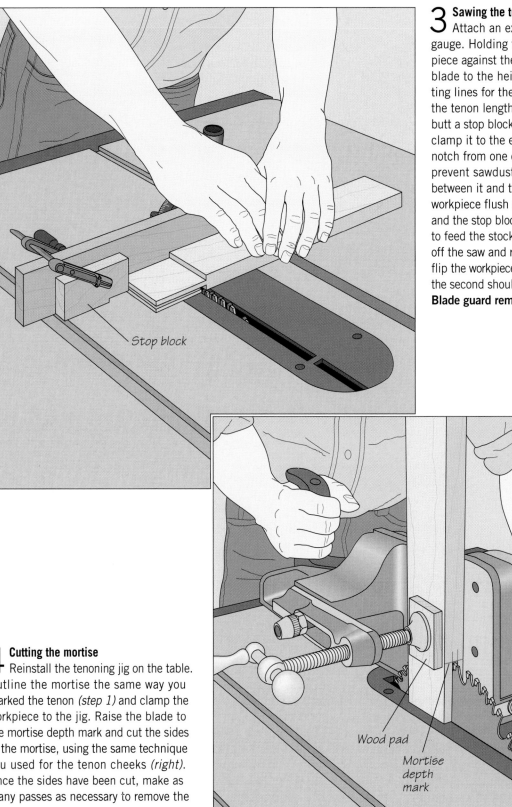

Stop block

3 Sawing the tenon shoulders
Attach an extension to your miter gauge. Holding the edge of the workpiece against the extension, adjust the blade to the height of one of the cutting lines for the tenon cheeks. Align the tenon length mark with the blade, butt a stop block against the stock, and clamp it to the extension; cut a small notch from one corner of the block to prevent sawdust from accumulating between it and the board. Holding the workpiece flush against the extension and the stop block, use the miter gauge to feed the stock into the blade. Turn off the saw and remove the waste, then flip the workpiece over and repeat to cut the second shoulder *(left)*. **(Caution: Blade guard removed for clarity.)**

4 Cutting the mortise
Reinstall the tenoning jig on the table. Outline the mortise the same way you marked the tenon *(step 1)* and clamp the workpiece to the jig. Raise the blade to the mortise depth mark and cut the sides of the mortise, using the same technique you used for the tenon cheeks *(right)*. Once the sides have been cut, make as many passes as necessary to remove the waste between them.

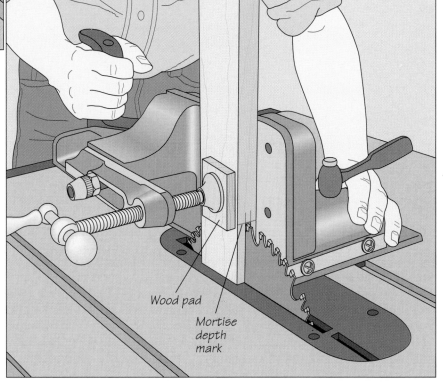

Wood pad

Mortise depth mark

A TABLE-SAW TENONING JIG

You can use the jig shown at right to cut both parts of an open mortise-and-tenon joint. Adapt the dimensions suggested in the illustration to customize the jig for your saw, if necessary.

Cut the jig fence and back from ¾-inch plywood and saw a 45° bevel at one end of each board; the pieces should be wider than the height of your saw's rip fence. Fasten two pieces together face-to-face to fashion the back, then use countersunk screws to attach the fence and back together in an L shape; make sure the fasteners will not be in the blade's path when you use the jig. Next, cut the brace from solid stock, bevel its ends, and attach it along the top edges of the fence and back, forming a triangle. Make the clamp by face gluing three pieces of ¾-inch plywood together and cutting the assembly into the shape shown. Use a hanger bolt, washer, and wing nut to attach

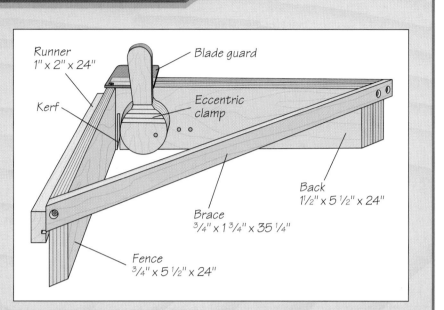

Runner
1" x 2" x 24"

Blade guard

Kerf

Eccentric
clamp

Brace
³/₄" x 1 ³/₄" x 35 ¼"

Back
1½" x 5 ½" x 24"

Fence
³/₄" x 5 ½" x 24"

the clamp to the jig back, leaving a gap between the edge of the clamp and the fence equal to the thickness of the stock you will use. Offset the bolt so the clamp can pivot eccentrically. (You can drill additional holes in the jig back to enable you to shift

the clamp to accommodate different stock thicknesses.) Next, cut the runner from solid wood and attach it to the jig fence so that the jig runs smoothly across the table without wobbling. For some models, you will have to mill a groove down the length of the runner, as shown, to fit the rip fence. Finally, cut a piece of clear plastic as a blade guard and screw it to the jig back flush with its front face.

To use the jig, set it on the saw table in front of the blade with the runner and fence straddling the rip fence. Clamp the workpiece in the jig and position the rip fence to align the cutting mark on the workpiece with the blade. Feed the jig into the cutting edge. (Your first use of the jig will produce a kerf in the back.) Flip the workpiece around and repeat to cut the other cheek *(left)*. (Refer to page 85 for instructions on making and using another style of jig that can cut open mortise-and-tenon joints.)

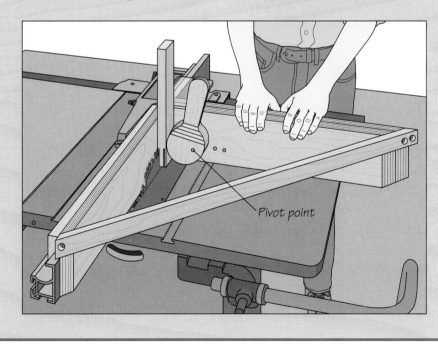

Pivot point

BLIND MORTISE-AND-TENON JOINTS

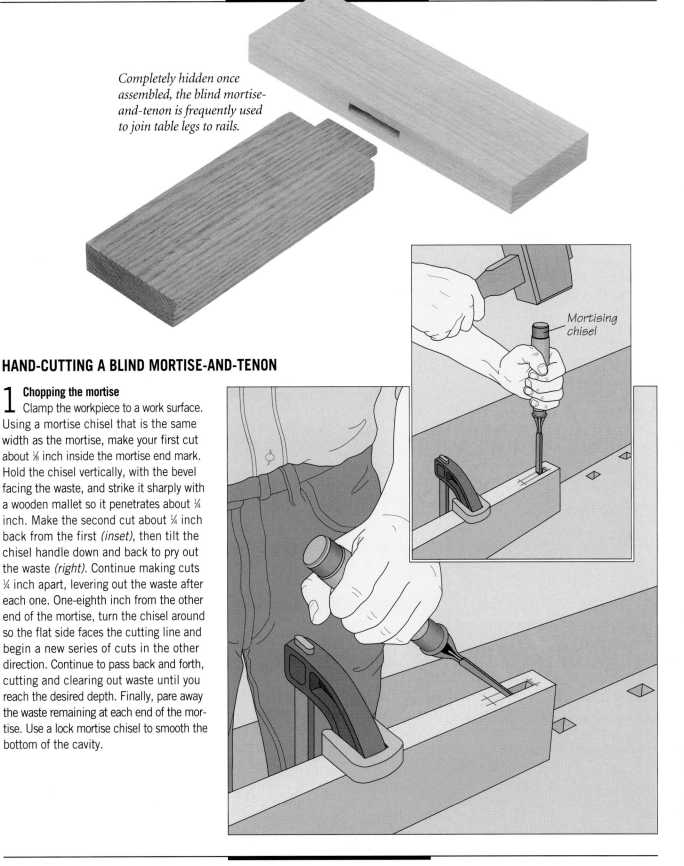

Completely hidden once assembled, the blind mortise-and-tenon is frequently used to join table legs to rails.

Mortising chisel

HAND-CUTTING A BLIND MORTISE-AND-TENON

1 Chopping the mortise
Clamp the workpiece to a work surface. Using a mortise chisel that is the same width as the mortise, make your first cut about ⅛ inch inside the mortise end mark. Hold the chisel vertically, with the bevel facing the waste, and strike it sharply with a wooden mallet so it penetrates about ¼ inch. Make the second cut about ¼ inch back from the first *(inset)*, then tilt the chisel handle down and back to pry out the waste *(right)*. Continue making cuts ¼ inch apart, levering out the waste after each one. One-eighth inch from the other end of the mortise, turn the chisel around so the flat side faces the cutting line and begin a new series of cuts in the other direction. Continue to pass back and forth, cutting and clearing out waste until you reach the desired depth. Finally, pare away the waste remaining at each end of the mortise. Use a lock mortise chisel to smooth the bottom of the cavity.

2 Cutting the tenon cheeks

Make a four-shouldered tenon by cutting the cheeks first, and then the shoulders. Mark a shoulder line all around the end of the workpiece and outline the cheeks with four lines that intersect on the board end. Secure the workpiece upright in a vise and cut down the cheek lines with a backsaw until you reach the shoulder line *(left)*.

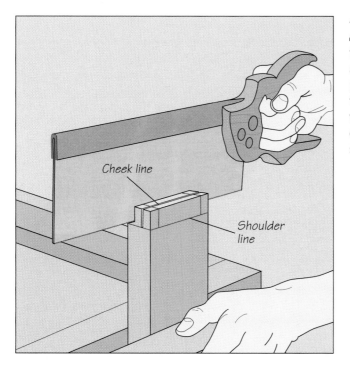

Cheek line

Shoulder line

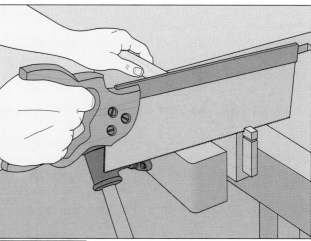

3 Sawing the tenon shoulders

To remove the waste from the tenon cheeks, clamp the workpiece in a miter box with the shoulder mark aligned with the 90° slot. Cut along the shoulder line on the face of the board *(left)*; turn the workpiece over and repeat the cut on the other side. To cut away the waste on the edges of the tenon, secure the work-piece end-up in the vise and cut the sides of the tenon, stopping at the shoulder line. Then, with the piece edge-up in the vise, saw along the shoulder line to the tenon. Finally, turn the board over in the vise and repeat to saw away the waste on the tenon's other edge *(above)*.

Miter box

CUTTING A MORTISE ON THE DRILL PRESS

1 Setting up the mortising attachment
A mortising attachment consists of a drill bit surrounded by a four-sided hollow chisel that squares the hole cut by the bit. After installing the attachment on your drill press, check whether the mortise chisel will be centered on the workpiece by securing a scrap board the same width and thickness as the workpiece to the mortising attachment fence. Bore a shallow cut into the board, then turn the board around end-for-end and make a second cut next to the first. The cuts should be aligned. If not, shift the fence by one-half the amount that the cuts are misaligned and repeat the test *(right)*. (In this illustration, the hold-down arm is raised for clarity.)

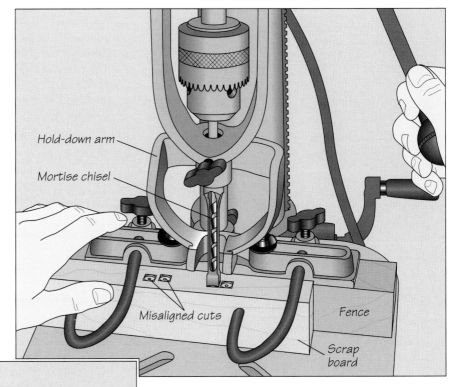

Hold-down arm

Mortise chisel

Misaligned cuts

Fence

Scrap board

SEQUENCE OF CUTS

Narrow mortise

Wide mortise

2 Drilling the mortise
Set the drilling depth to the mortise depth and secure the workpiece to the fence, centering the mortise outline under the chisel. Adjust the hold-down arm and rods so the stock can slide freely along the fence. Make a cut at each end of the outline, then a series of staggered cuts, following the sequence shown above to complete the mortise. Mark a single row of cuts if you are using a chisel equal in width to the mortise, or two parallel rows if the mortise is too wide to be cut in a single pass.

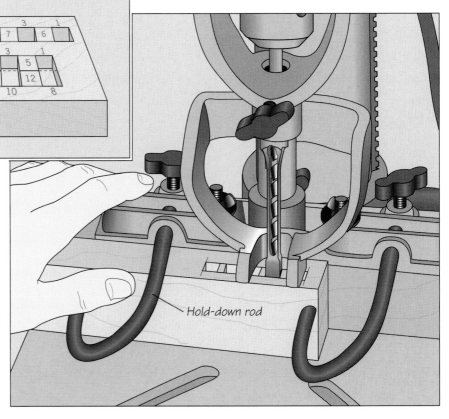

Hold-down rod

WEDGED THROUGH MORTISE-AND-TENON JOINTS

Wedges can tighten and strengthen a through mortise-and-tenon. The wedged mortise-and-tenon joint is made by cutting slots in the end of the tenon, and driving wedges into the cuts after the tenon is fitted into the mortise. The wedges push the tenon more tightly against the mortise walls. By using wedges cut from contrasting hardwood, the joint can lend a decorative touch to a piece of furniture.

MAKING A WEDGED THROUGH MORTISE-AND-TENON

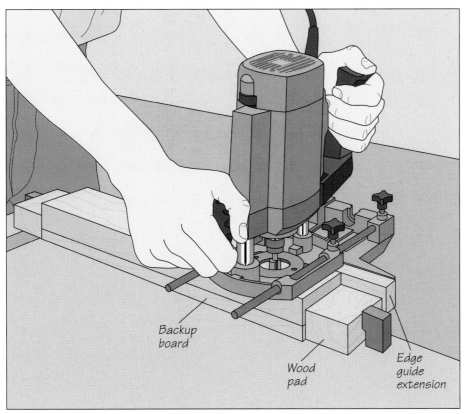

Backup board

Wood pad

Edge guide extension

1 Routing out the mortise
Secure the workpiece between two bench dogs, using wood pads to protect the stock. Since you will be cutting a through mortise, place a backup board under the workpiece to protect your benchtop. Fit a plunge router with a straight bit the same diameter as the width of the mortise, then set the depth of cut. As this is typically a deep cut, several passes will be necessary. Attach a wooden extension to the fence of a commercial edge guide to increase its bearing surface, then fasten the guide to the router base plate. Center the bit over the mortise outline and adjust the extension so it rests flush against the workpiece. Holding the router firmly, plunge the bit into the stock at one end of the mortise outline, then feed the bit to the other end. When the mortise is cut to the full depth, square its corners with a chisel.

ROUTING DEEP THROUGH MORTISES

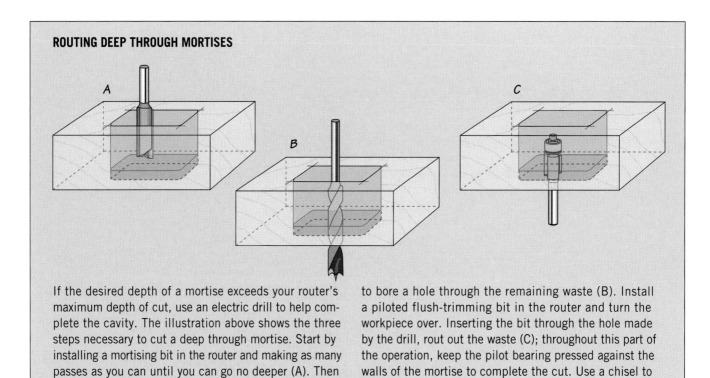

If the desired depth of a mortise exceeds your router's maximum depth of cut, use an electric drill to help complete the cavity. The illustration above shows the three steps necessary to cut a deep through mortise. Start by installing a mortising bit in the router and making as many passes as you can until you can go no deeper (A). Then use the drill with a bit that is larger than your router bit to bore a hole through the remaining waste (B). Install a piloted flush-trimming bit in the router and turn the workpiece over. Inserting the bit through the hole made by the drill, rout out the waste (C); throughout this part of the operation, keep the pilot bearing pressed against the walls of the mortise to complete the cut. Use a chisel to square the mortise corners.

2 Sawing the slots in the tenon
Cut a four-shouldered tenon *(page 95)*, making sure the tenon is long enough to pass completely through the mating piece. Clamp the stock upright in a vise and use a backsaw to cut two kerfs into the end of the tenon *(right)*, stopping ¼ inch short of the shoulder; space the kerfs in from each edge of the tenon a distance roughly equal to the thickness of the tenon.

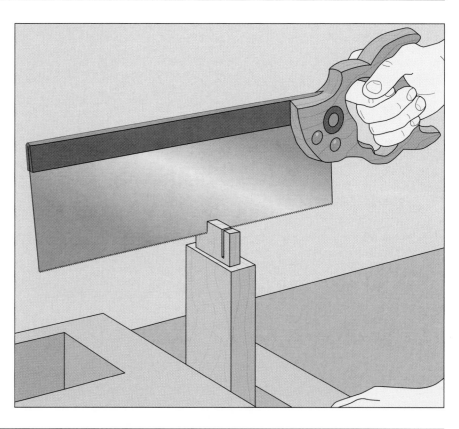

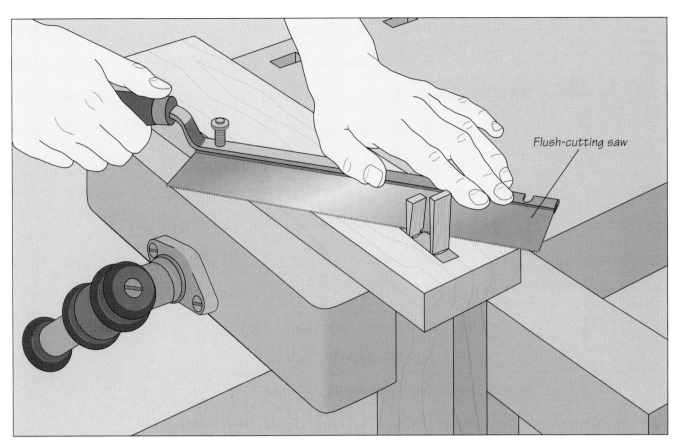

Flush-cutting saw

3 Inserting the wedges

Saw two hardwood wedges to fit into the slots cut in step 2; make them as wide as the tenon, but a few inches longer, and no thicker than $\frac{1}{4}$ inch at the broad end. Glue up the joint, then secure the pieces in a vise with the end of the tenon facing up. Apply some glue to the wedges and use a mallet to drive them into the kerfs as far as they will go; tap the wedges alternately to keep them equal. Once the glue has dried, use a flush-cutting saw to trim the wedges even with the end of the tenon (above), then sand the surface smooth.

SHOP TIP

Tightening up a loose tenon
Use a strip of veneer to snug up a loose mortise-and-tenon joint. Before gluing up the joint, cut the veneer to the same length and width as the tenon. Assemble the joint with the veneer wedged in between the tenon and the mortise, or kerf the tenon along its length and insert a wedge as described above. If a tenon is so loose that a single wedge or piece of veneer will not do, cut a new tenon.

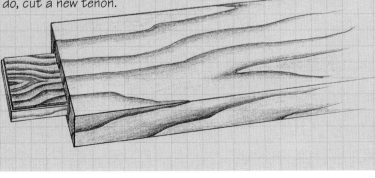

A MORTISING JIG FOR THE ROUTER

Use the jig shown at right to secure the workpiece and guide your router as you cut a mortise. The dimensions suggested in the illustration will suit most routers. Cut the jig base and sides from ¾-inch plywood. Fasten three pieces together for the base. Attach the sides to the base with countersunk screws, making sure the pieces are perfectly square to each other. Fashion each stop block from solid wood, rout a groove in one face ⅜ inch deep and ¾ inch wide, then cut a 4-inch-long slot to accept a ¼-inch hanger bolt. Mount the bolts 3 inches from each end of one side, slip the stop blocks in place and fix them with washers and wing nuts.

To use the jig, set the workpiece on the base with the mortise outline between the stop blocks and one surface flush against the side with the blocks. Place a shim under the stock so its top surface is butted against the blocks, then clamp the workpiece to the jig and secure the jig in a vise. To set up the router for the cut, install a straight bit the same diameter as the width of the mortise, set the depth of cut and attach a commercial edge guide to the base plate, center the bit over the mortise outline and adjust the guide so it rests flush against the opposite side of the jig. Adjust each stop block by aligning the bit with the end of the mortise outline, butting the block against the router's base plate and tightening the wing nut. After confirming the position of the blocks and edge guide, grip the router firmly, butt the edge guide against the

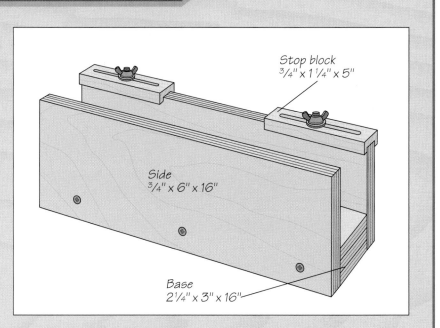

Stop block
¾" x 1¼" x 5"

Side
¾" x 6" x 16"

Base
2¼" x 3" x 16"

jig, press the base plate against one stop block and plunge the bit into the work. Hold the edge guide against the jig as you draw the router through the cut until it contacts the other stop block *(below)*.

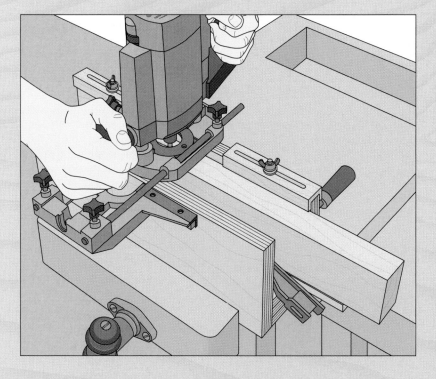

HAUNCHED MORTISE-AND-TENON JOINTS

The haunched mortise-and-tenon features mating notches cut in the tenon cheek and mortise. The result is a joint that provides more resistance to twist than the blind mortise-and-tenon. The haunched joint is often used in frame-and-panel construction, where the haunch fills the end of the groove that is cut for the panel, eliminating the need for stopped grooves.

MAKING A HAUNCHED MORTISE-AND-TENON

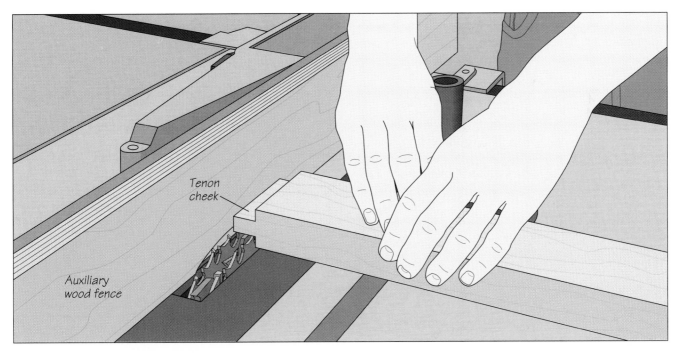

Tenon cheek

Auxiliary wood fence

1 Cutting the tenon cheeks
On a table saw, install a dado head slightly wider than the length of the tenon, then attach and notch an auxiliary fence *(page 71)*. Set the width of cut equal to the tenon length; adjust the cutting height to leave a tenon the same thickness as the width of the mortise chisel or router bit you will be using. Feed the stock face-down into the dado head, holding the workpiece firmly against the fence and the miter gauge. Turn the workpiece over and repeat the cut on the other side *(above)*.

2 Cutting the haunch

Set the blade height to cut a shoulder on the inside edge of the workpiece. Once the cut is made, advance the rip fence to cut the haunch in the tenon. The haunch should be approximately as wide as the tenon is thick. (If you are making the rails and stiles of a frame-and-panel assembly, the width of the haunch should equal the depth of the groove for the panel.) With the workpiece on edge, use the fence and the miter gauge to guide it over the dado head *(right)*. If there is no panel groove in the mating workpiece, you must next notch the mortise *(step 3)*.

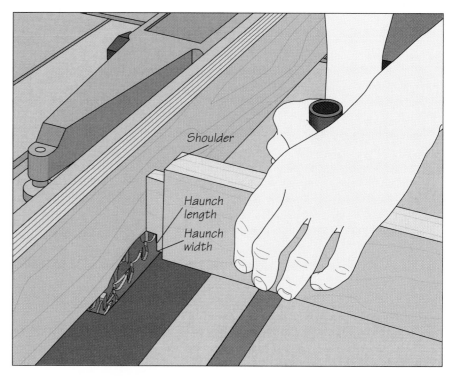

Shoulder

Haunch length

Haunch width

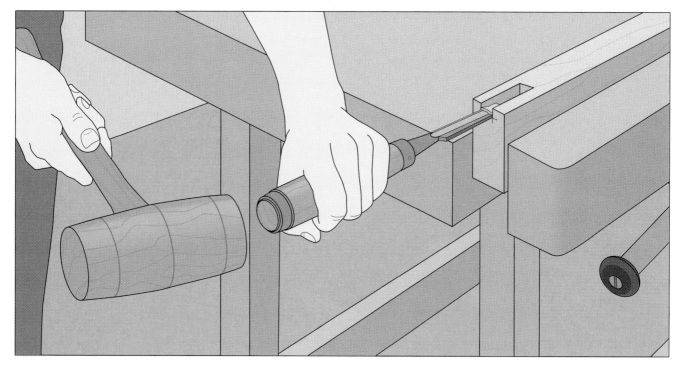

3 Notching the mortise for the haunch

Secure the workpiece in a vise and chop out a mortise as you would for a blind tenon *(page 94)*. Use the haunched tenon as a guide to outline the width and depth of the notch on the workpiece, then kerf the edges of the outline with a backsaw. Use a chisel to split off the waste in ⅛-inch layers between the cuts until you reach the required depth. Holding the blade bevel-up and parallel to the surface, strike the handle with a mallet *(above)*. Pare the sides of the notch with the chisel, if necessary.

ANGLED MORTISE-AND-TENON JOINTS

Angled tenons are often used in building chairs to get around the joinery problem caused by seats that are wider at the front than at the back—a traditional design feature. To accommodate the angled side rails, tenons must be cut at opposite ends at opposing angles, while the tenon shoulders must be parallel to each other. Although the tenon is tricky to mark out and produce, it fits into a standard mortise.

CUTTING ANGLED TENONS

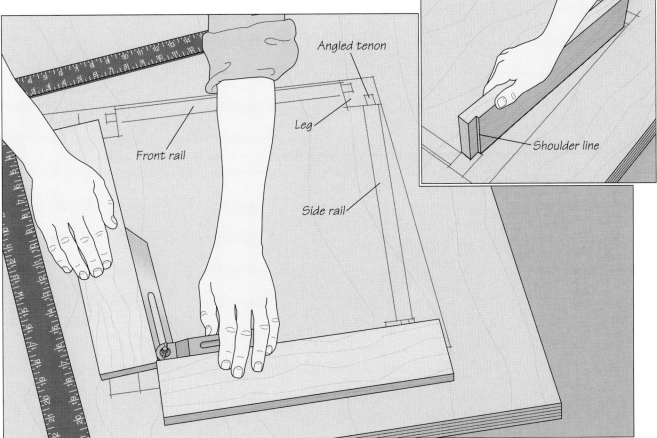

Angled tenon

Leg

Front rail

Side rail

Shoulder line

1 Planning the job

To mark out angled tenons, sketch the project full-size on a piece of plywood or hardboard. In this example, the underside of a chair frame has been drawn, including the legs and rails. Standard blind tenons are needed on the front and back rails; angled tenons must be cut on the side rails; and standard mortises must be chopped out in the legs. To set the blade angle on your table saw for cutting the angled tenon cheeks, align two boards along one corner of the outline and adjust a sliding bevel to the angle formed by the boards *(above)*. Install a dado head

and transfer the angle to the blades. Install and notch an auxiliary fence *(page 71)* and set a cutting width of ¾ inch and a height of ⅛ inch. Feed a scrap piece the same size as your stock face-down into the dado head to make test cuts across both ends. Then position the test piece on your outline *(inset)*. The shoulder lines on the piece and the drawing should line up; if not, increase the cutting width and make another set of cuts, continuing until the shoulders align. Adjust the cutting height until the tenon cheeks on the piece line up with the drawing.

Shoulder line

2 Cutting the tenon cheeks

Once the cutting width and height of the dado blade have been properly set, put the test piece aside and make the cuts on your workpiece. Use the miter gauge and fence to guide the board for one pass, then turn the board over and repeat the cut at the other end *(above)*. To line up the saw cuts for the other side of the cheeks, set the workpiece on edge and use the sliding bevel to extend the shoulder line across the edge of the board *(inset)*. Then move the rip fence to the other side of the dado head, and reposition and notch the auxiliary fence accordingly. Align the shoulder mark with the outside blade of the dado head and butt the fence against the end of the stock. Cut the remaining cheeks *(right)* the same way you produced the first two. (Make these cuts on the test piece first, and then adjust the cutting width and height, if necessary.)

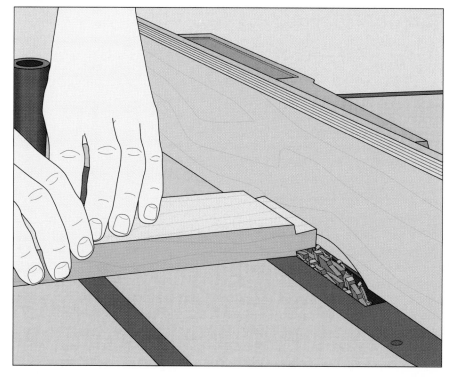

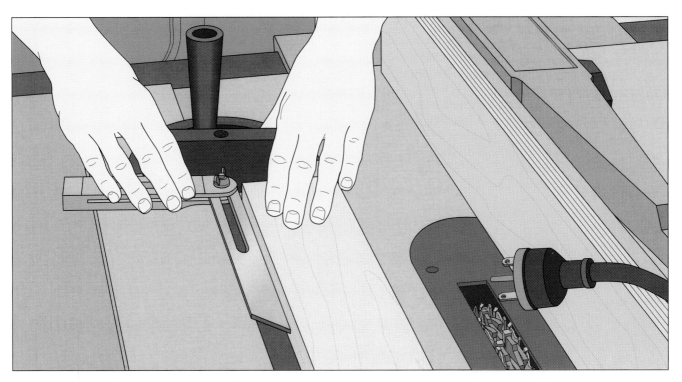

3 Setting up the saw for the tenon shoulders
Adjust the angle of the dado head to 90°. Holding a board parallel to the miter slot, use the sliding bevel to set the miter gauge to the same angle used to adjust the blades in step 1 *(above)*. Butt the workpiece on edge against the miter gauge. The shoulder should be parallel to the rip fence; if not, flip the workpiece over to its other edge. Set the width of cut to the width of the cheek and adjust the dado head to the desired cutting height.

4 Cutting the tenon shoulders
Like the tenon cheeks, the shoulders are cut in two steps. For the first set of cuts, guide the workpiece on edge using the miter gauge and fence *(left)*, then turn the board end-for-end and repeat the cut. To make the second set of cuts, use the sliding bevel as in step 3 to angle the miter gauge in the opposite direction. Cut the last two shoulders on the other edge the same way you made the first two.

TUSK TENON JOINTS

The tusk tenon is commonly used to join the legs and stretcher of a trestle table. The tenon extends beyond the through mortise so that a tusk-like wedge can be inserted to lock the joint while enabling it to be disassembled. Depending on the length and width of the tenon, the wedge can be inserted through either its thickness or its width.

MAKING A TUSK TENON JOINT

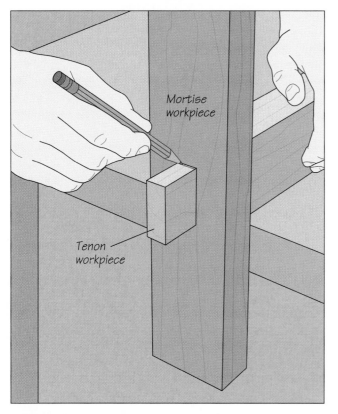

Mortise workpiece

Tenon workpiece

1 Marking the location of the tenon wedge
Cut a four-shouldered tenon *(page 94)*, but make it long enough to extend from the mortise workpiece by at least 1 inch. This will provide sufficient stock to resist being split by the wedge. Cut a through mortise to accommodate the tenon and assemble the joint. Then, holding the pieces together on a work surface, mark a line along the top of the cheek where the tenon emerges from the mortise *(above)*.

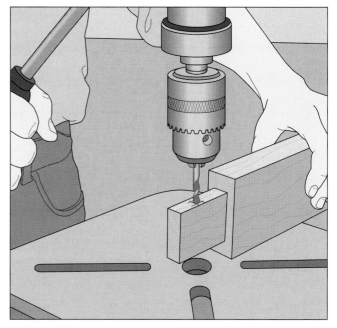

2 Drilling the hole for the wedge
Disassemble the joint and make a drilling mark $\frac{1}{16}$ inch on the shoulder side of the scribed line; this will ensure a tight fit when the wedge is driven into place. Set a mortise gauge to one-third the thickness of the tenon and use the gauge to outline the hole in the middle third of the top cheek, bordering on your mark. Using a bit slightly smaller in diameter than the outline, bore the hole through the tenon on the drill press *(above)*.

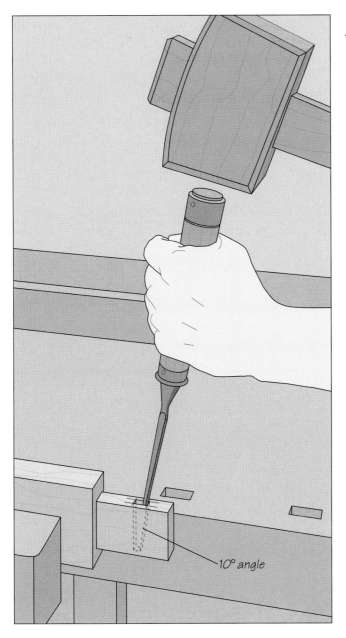

10° angle

3 Angling the wedge hole
Enlarge and square the hole you drilled to accommodate the wedge. Holding a mortise chisel at a 10° angle away from the tenon shoulders, cut a tapered slot, as indicated by the dotted lines in the illustration. Chop out the waste as you would cut a blind mortise *(page 94)*.

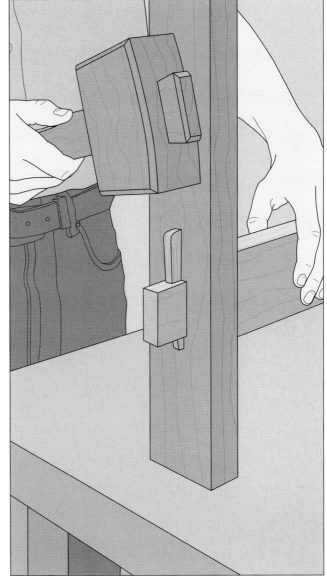

4 Inserting the tenon wedge
Cut a triangular hardwood wedge that is tapered to fit the slot you chopped out in step 3; its length can be up to twice the tenon width. To assemble the joint, slide the tenon into the mortise and strike the wedge firmly with a mallet until the joint is tight *(right)*. Do not use glue, as this joint is designed to be disassembled.

TWIN MORTISE-AND-TENON JOINTS

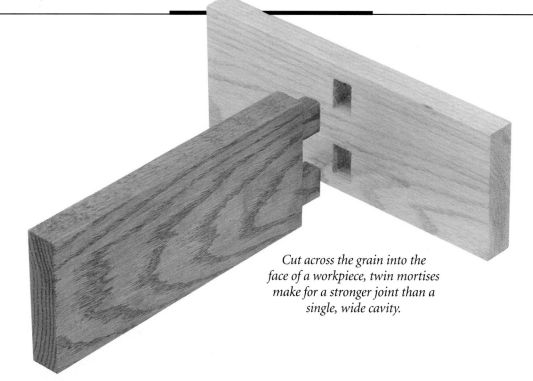

*Cut across the grain into the
face of a workpiece, twin mortises
make for a stronger joint than a
single, wide cavity.*

MAKING A TWIN MORTISE-AND-TENON JOINT

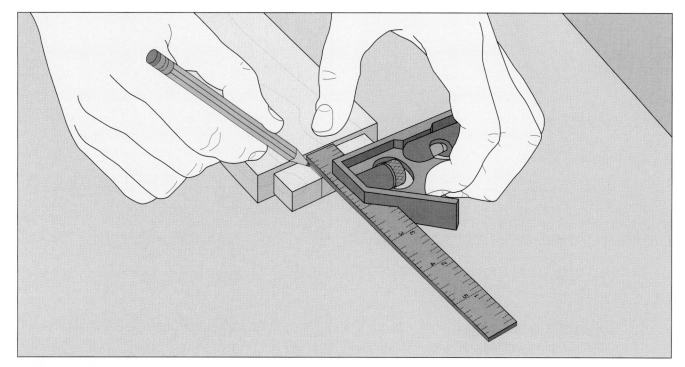

1 Laying out the tenons
Begin by cutting an ordinary four-shouldered through tenon as you would for a wedged
joint *(page 97)*. Then use a combination square to mark out the twin tenons *(above)*.
The normal practice is to divide the tenon into thirds, making the width of the tenons and
the gap between them the same. Mark the middle waste portion with Xs to avoid confusion.

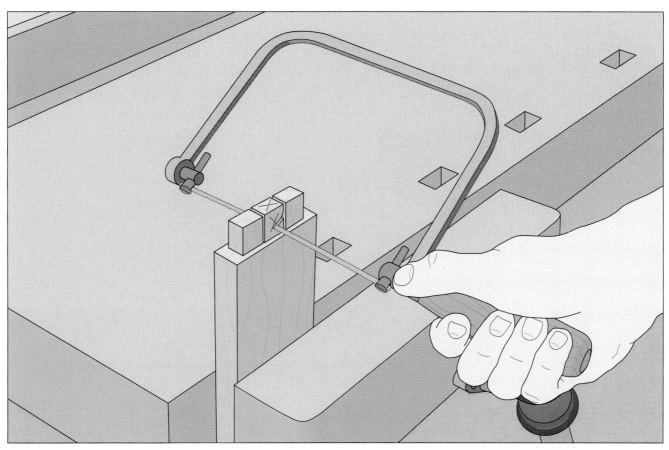

2 Cutting out the waste

Clamp the tenon workpiece end-up in a vise and cut along the edges of the waste section with a backsaw, stopping at the shoulder. Then use a coping saw to remove the waste *(above)*, taking care to avoid cutting into the shoulder. Use a chisel to pare to the line.

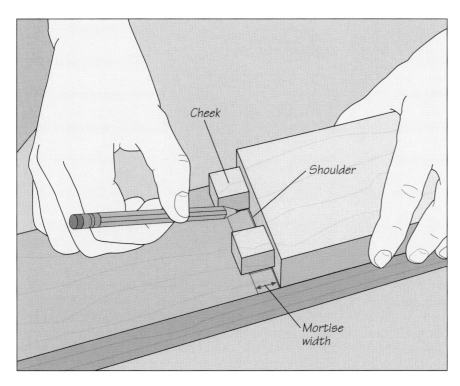

Cheek

Shoulder

Mortise width

3 Laying out the mortises

Draw two lines representing the width of the twin mortises on the face of the mortise workpiece, then set both work-pieces on a work surface with the tenon workpiece on top. Align the tenon shoulder with one of the marked lines and outline the two mortises using the tenon cheeks as guides *(left)*, then remove the waste as you would for any deep through mortise *(page 98)*.

ROUND MORTISE-AND-TENON JOINTS

Round tenons are often produced on turned workpieces such as chair legs and rungs with the help of a lathe or band saw, but they can also be cut in square stock with a drill press and tenon cutter. The mortise is also bored on a drill press.

MAKING A ROUND MORTISE-AND-TENON

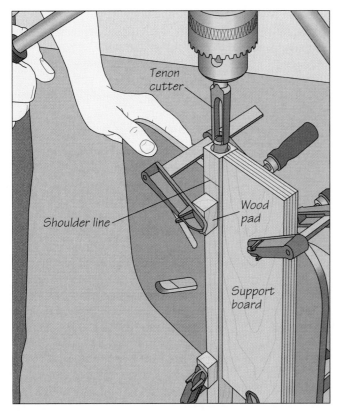

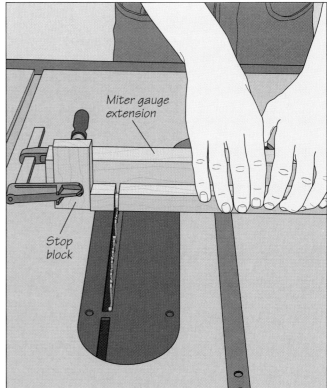

Cutting a round tenon on a square workpiece

Make a round tenon in two steps, starting on the drill press and then removing the waste on the table saw. Install a tenon cutter on the drill press and tilt the table to 90°. Clamp the workpiece and a support board to the table, using pads to protect the wood, then bore the hole to the depth of the shoulder *(above, left)*. On the table saw, adjust the cutting height to cut away the waste encircling the tenon and screw a board as an extension to the miter gauge. Align the shoulder line with the blade, butt a stop block against the end of the workpiece and clamp it to the extension. Holding the stock flush against the extension and the stop block, make a cut on each edge of the workpiece *(above, right)* to sever the waste. Make the mating mortise on the drill press.

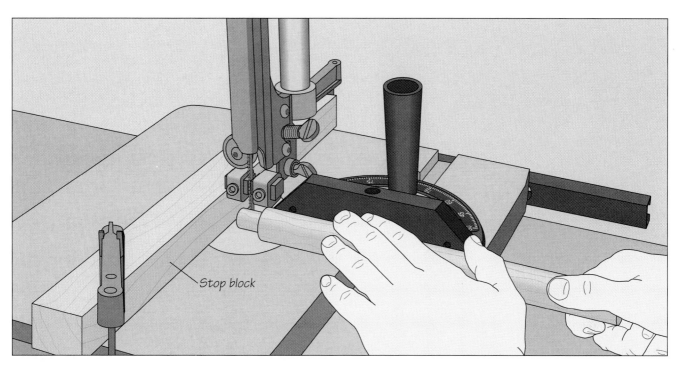

Stop block

SHOP TIP

A round-tenon jig for the router table
The simple plywood jig shown here enables you to
rout round tenons in turned pieces. Make the
L-shaped jig higher than your router table's
fence, with a brace that holds the workpiece
snugly. Install a straight
bit in the router and an
insert in the table that surrounds the cutter as
closely as possible.
Adjust the cutter
height to the
length of the
tenon. Then clamp
the jig to the
center of the fence
and set them for a
partial cut. Holding
the workpiece securely in the jig
with one hand, turn on the router and lower the stock onto the
bit while turning it clockwise, against bit rotation. Advance
the fence 1/8 inch at a time until the tenon is completed.

Cutting a round tenon in turned stock
A band saw can be used to fashion a
round tenon in a turned workpiece.
Clamp the miter gauge to the table so
that the gap between its face and the
cutting edge of the blade is the same
as the desired depth of tenon shoulder.
Align the shoulder line on the workpiece
with the blade, and clamp a board
against the end of the stock as a stop
block; make sure the board is parallel to
the miter gauge slot. Cut the tenon in
two steps. First, rotate the workpiece
clockwise on the table and miter gauge
while cutting a series of concentric kerfs
1/8 inch apart from the end of the stock
to the shoulder line. Then clear the
waste by pushing the workpiece across
the blade while rotating it *(above)*. Cut
deep shoulders in two or three passes,
moving the miter gauge away from the
blade between each pass.

DOVETAIL AND BOX JOINTS

Fitted with a straight bit, a table-mounted router cuts the notches for a box joint. A hardwood key glued into the miter gauge extension guarantees uniform spacing between the cuts.

The dovetail joint was developed centuries ago to compensate for the unreliable adhesives available at the time. Compared to the costly, hand-wrought fasteners then available, the interlocking pins and tails of the dovetail offered a practical and attractive solution to a construction problem. Although its execution requires considerable skill and time, no joint can match the dovetail's ability to hold a corner joint together without additional reinforcement.

Modern adhesives have made the dovetail almost unnecessary, but it is still called upon to hold the corners of carcases and drawers together. Today, the rationale for using it is esthetic; the dovetail is visual shorthand for durability and woodworking skill.

The joint consists of tapered pins that fit around flared tails resembling the tail feathers of a dove, which gives the joint its name. The joint provides good long-grain gluing surface, which adds to its strength.

Several varieties of the dovetail joint are shown in this chapter. The through dovetail *(page 118)* is the strongest, since the tails and pins are cut through the full thickness of the boards. The curved and outlined through dovetail joints, shown on pages 126 and 128 respectively, are decorative variations of the basic design. Half-blind *(page 130)* and blind dovetail joints provide comparable strength while concealing end grain. This feature makes the half-blind joint a favorite for attaching drawer fronts.

Box and finger joints came into extensive use in the 19th Century for production-line assemblies like telephone boxes, sewing machines, and packing crates. They are easy to cut and, although they are not self-locking, these joints provide a large area of long-grain contact for gluing.

Both dovetail and box joints can be cut by hand or machine. Box and finger joints can be cut equally well with the router, the table saw *(page 132)*, or the radial arm saw *(page 134)*. Hand-cutting a dovetail joint is often considered a rite of passage for apprentice woodworkers. It takes more time and effort than machine cutting, but the technique allows complete control over the layout of the joint. Dovetails can be produced quickly and accurately on the router using a commercial jig. In many cases, however, the spacing and angle of the pins and tails cannot be varied, and some woodworkers find that the resulting joint lacks the esthetic appeal of a handcut joint.

A coping saw is used to cut away the waste between the pins of a dovetail joint. The narrow blade allows the saw to curve sharply from the side of the pins to the shoulder line. The remaining waste will be pared away with a chisel.

A SELECTION OF DOVETAIL AND BOX JOINTS

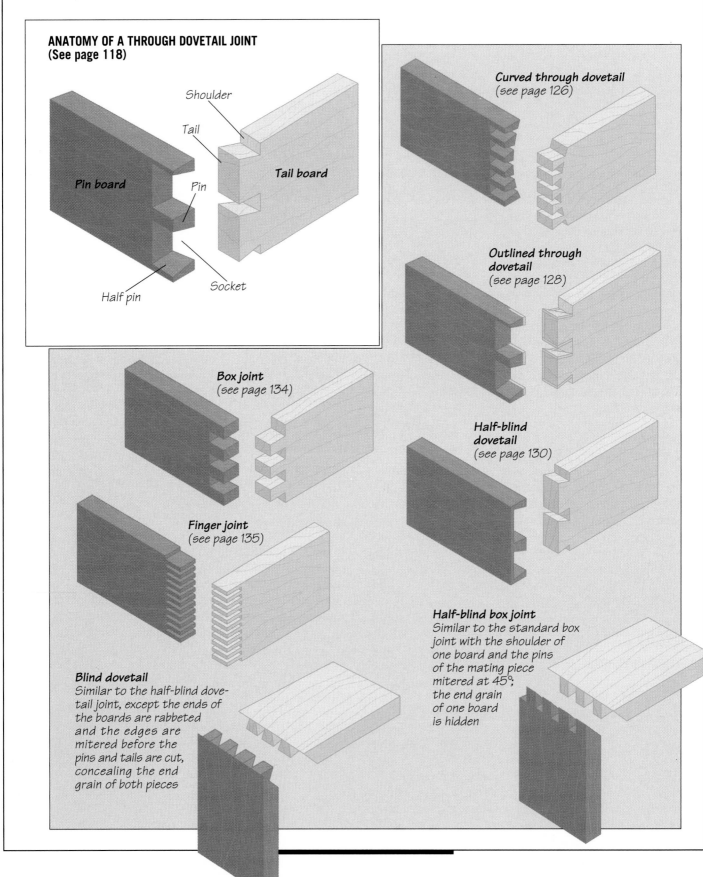

ANATOMY OF A THROUGH DOVETAIL JOINT
(See page 118)

Shoulder

Tail

Pin board

Tail board

Pin

Half pin

Socket

Curved through dovetail
(see page 126)

Outlined through dovetail
(see page 128)

Box joint
(see page 134)

Half-blind dovetail
(see page 130)

Finger joint
(see page 135)

Blind dovetail
Similar to the half-blind dovetail joint, except the ends of the boards are rabbeted and the edges are mitered before the pins and tails are cut, concealing the end grain of both pieces

Half-blind box joint
Similar to the standard box joint with the shoulder of one board and the pins of the mating piece mitered at 45°; the end grain of one board is hidden

DESIGNING AND MARKING DOVETAILS

Spacing and angling the pins

The space between the pins and tails of a dovetail and the slope angle of the pins affect both the strength of the joint and its esthetic appeal. Several common spacing ratios—expressed as tail-to-pin size—are shown at right. The 1-to-1 ratio creates the strongest joint, but results in the least attractive layout. The other spacing ratios illustrated are more attractive and virtually as sturdy. The 3-to-1 ratio is a good choice for a joint that will feature prominently on a piece. Pin-spacing ratios greater than 3-to-1 are weak and should be avoided.

There is less latitude in marking the angle of the pins. Too small an angle will prevent the pieces from locking together, allowing the joint to pull apart; too great an angle stresses the corners of the tails, causing them to break off. For softwoods, a ratio of 1:6 or 80° is required; for hardwoods, the ratio normally used is 1:8 or 83° *(inset)*. Using a dovetail square to mark the pins will automatically give you the correct angle.

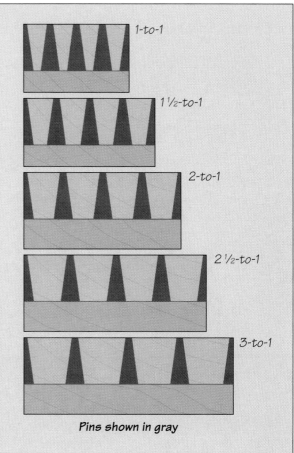

1-to-1

1 ½-to-1

2-to-1

2 ½-to-1

3-to-1

Pins shown in gray

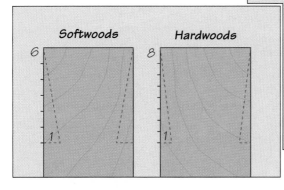

Softwoods   Hardwoods

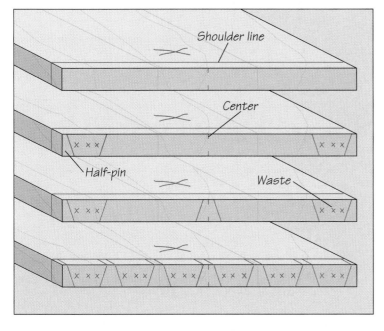

Shoulder line

Center

Half-pin

Waste

Outlining the pins

The construction of a dovetail joint begins with laying out, marking and cutting the pins, then using them to outline the tails on the mating board. Begin laying out the joint by marking the outside face of the workpiece with a big X, then use a cutting gauge to scribe the shoulder line of the joint *(page 118)*. Next, use a dovetail square to lay out the pins on the ends of the board as shown in the sequence at left. (See page 119 for instructions on making a dovetail square in the shop.) Begin with half-pins at each edge, making sure the narrow ends of the pins are on the outside face of the board. Next outline the waste sections adjacent to the half-pins. On a wide workpiece, such as the one in the illustration, you next mark the center of the board end. Outline a pin at the center mark, then outline the remaining pins, marking all the waste sections with Xs.

JIGS AND ACCESSORIES

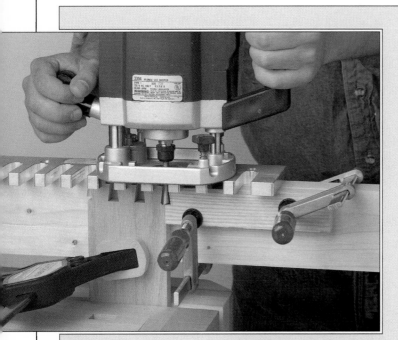

Commercial dovetail jigs are ideal for producing a series of identical joints. This model consists of two templates fastened to backup boards. The workpiece is secured to the jig and a stop block helps with positioning for repeat cuts. Here, a router fitted with a dovetail bit moves in and out of the slots of the tail board template.

Box joint jig
Plastic jig attached to a router table for cutting finger or box joints; ridge in center of jig functions as a key to make precise repeat cuts

Dovetail templates
A set of two fixed templates fastened to backup boards to rout through dovetail joints; one template is for pins and the other for tails. Three models are available for routing different-sized pins; uses top-piloted bits

Interchangeable-template jig
With the use of interchangeable templates, jig allows router to cut dovetail and box joints with a single setup; comes with guide bushing and router bits

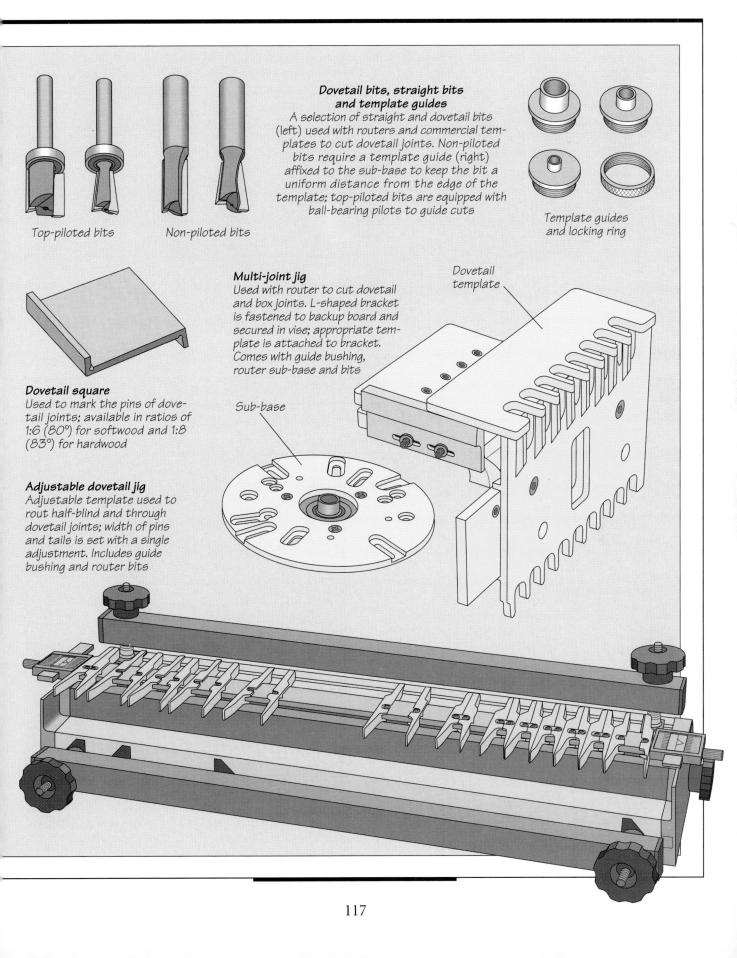

Top-piloted bits   **Non-piloted bits**

Dovetail bits, straight bits and template guides

A selection of straight and dovetail bits (left) used with routers and commercial templates to cut dovetail joints. Non-piloted bits require a template guide (right) affixed to the sub-base to keep the bit a uniform distance from the edge of the template; top-piloted bits are equipped with ball-bearing pilots to guide cuts

Template guides and locking ring

Dovetail square
Used to mark the pins of dovetail joints; available in ratios of 1:6 (80°) for softwood and 1:8 (83°) for hardwood

Adjustable dovetail jig
Adjustable template used to rout half-blind and through dovetail joints; width of pins and tails is set with a single adjustment. Includes guide bushing and router bits

Multi-joint jig
Used with router to cut dovetail and box joints. L-shaped bracket is fastened to backup board and secured in vise; appropriate template is attached to bracket. Comes with guide bushing, router sub-base and bits

Dovetail template

Sub-base

THROUGH DOVETAIL JOINTS

Combining mechanical strength with a distinctive appearance, the through dovetail joint is frequently used in fine furniture to join drawers and carcase corners.

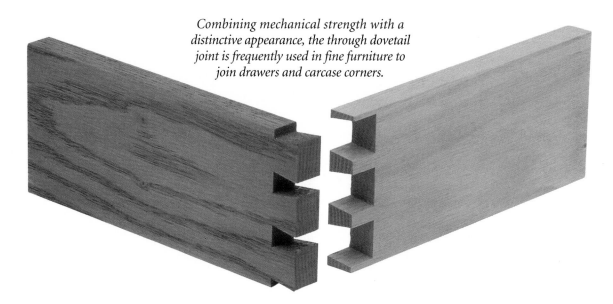

CUTTING A THROUGH DOVETAIL BY HAND

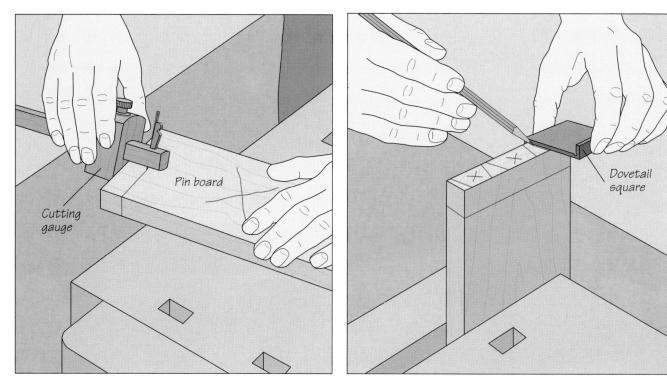

Pin board

Cutting gauge

Dovetail square

1 Laying out the pins
Mark the outside face of the board with an X. Then set a cutting gauge to the thickness of the stock and scribe a line along the end of the board to mark the shoulder of the pins and tails *(above, left)*. Next, secure the stock end-up in a vise and use a dovetail square to outline the pins on the end of the board. You can follow the sequence illustrated on page 115,

but for stock of the width shown above—typical for a drawer—a half-pin at each edge and two evenly spaced pins in between will make a strong and attractive joint *(above, right)*. Mark the waste sections with an X as you go. Finally, use a combination square to extend all the dovetail marks down both faces of the board to the shoulder lines.

DOVETAIL SQUARE

Instead of buying a dovetail square, you can make your own by face-gluing four pieces of scrap wood together at the required dovetail angle.

Cut the pieces of the jig about 6 or 8 inches long and 1½ inches wide.

To prepare the pieces, adjust the miter gauge of your table saw to the appropriate angle—1:6 (or 80°) for softwood or 1:8 (or 83°) for hardwood. Then make a cut across the center of the piece, slicing it in half. Make the same cut at both ends of the marking guide. Spread some glue on all the contacting faces and assemble the jig, butting the cut ends of the middle pieces against the marking guide, while aligning their edges with the other two boards of the crosspiece above and below. Trim the ends of the middle pieces flush with the crosspiece.

To use the jig, lay the marking guide across the end of the pin board while butting the edge of the crosspiece against the face of the board.

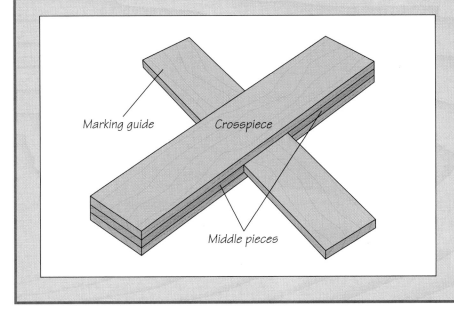

Marking guide

Crosspiece

Middle pieces

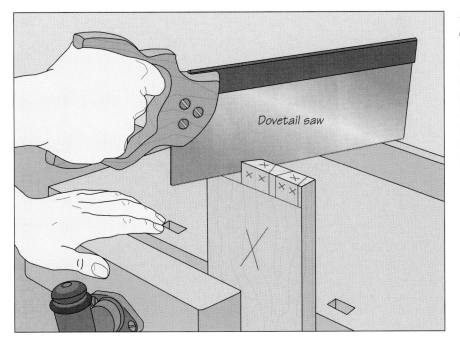

Dovetail saw

2 Cutting the pins

Leave the pin board in the vise with its outside face toward you. Use a dovetail saw to cut along the edges of the pins, aligning the saw blade just to the waste side of the cutting line. Cut all the right-hand edges first *(left)*, then complete the left-hand edges. Use smooth, even strokes, taking care to keep the blade perpendicular as you cut to the shoulder lines.

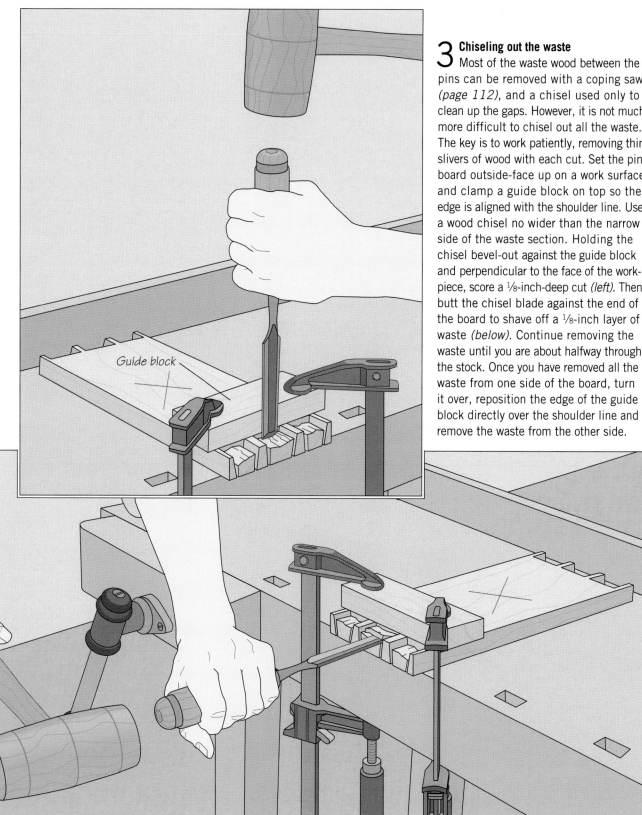

Guide block

3 Chiseling out the waste

Most of the waste wood between the pins can be removed with a coping saw *(page 112)*, and a chisel used only to clean up the gaps. However, it is not much more difficult to chisel out all the waste. The key is to work patiently, removing thin slivers of wood with each cut. Set the pin board outside-face up on a work surface and clamp a guide block on top so the edge is aligned with the shoulder line. Use a wood chisel no wider than the narrow side of the waste section. Holding the chisel bevel-out against the guide block and perpendicular to the face of the work-piece, score a ⅛-inch-deep cut *(left)*. Then butt the chisel blade against the end of the board to shave off a ⅛-inch layer of waste *(below)*. Continue removing the waste until you are about halfway through the stock. Once you have removed all the waste from one side of the board, turn it over, reposition the edge of the guide block directly over the shoulder line and remove the waste from the other side.

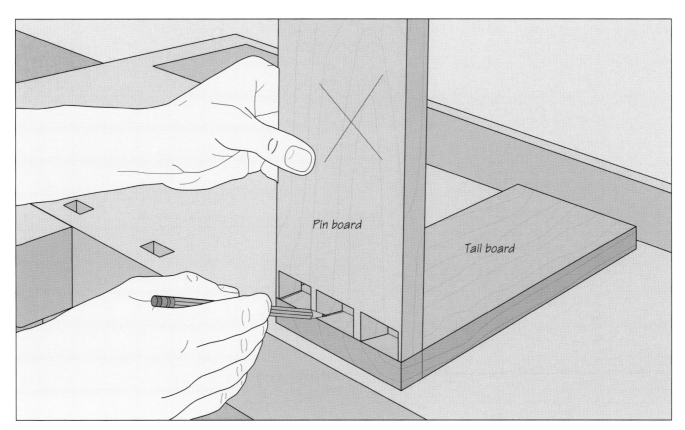

Pin board

Tail board

4 Laying out the tails
Set the tail board outside-face down on the work surface. Hold the pin board end-down with its inside face aligned with the shoulder line of the tail board, making certain the edges of the boards are flush. Outline the tails with a pencil *(above)*, then use a try square to extend the lines on the end of the board. Mark all the waste sections with Xs.

SHOP TIP

Marking tails on wide boards
Panels and wide boards may be too cumbersome to hold steady while you are outlining the tails on a tail board. The setup shown here makes the task easy. Set the tail board outside-face down on a work surface and clamp a guide block on top of it with the edge of the block flush with the shoulder line. Then hold the end of the pin board against the guide block with its outside face away from the tail board. Fasten a handscrew to the pin board and use another clamp to hold it firmly in position while you outline the tails.

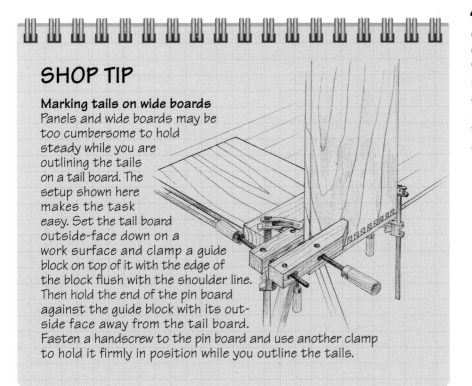

5 Cutting the tails and removing the waste

Use a dovetail saw to cut the tails the same way you cut the pins *(step 2)*. Angling the board *(left)*, rather than the saw, makes for easier cutting. Secure the board so that the right-hand edges of the tails are vertical. Saw smoothly and evenly along the edges of the tails, stopping at the shoulder line. Reposition the board in the vise to cut the left-hand edges. Once all the saw cuts have been made, remove the waste with a chisel as in step 3.

6 Dry-fitting the drawer

Before gluing up the joint, assemble it to check the fit. Stand the pin board on end on a work surface, then align the tail board with it. Press the joint together by hand as far as it will go, then use the mallet to tap the boards the rest of the way into position *(right)*. To avoid marring the pins and tails, close the joint evenly along its entire length. The pins and tails should fit snugly, requiring only a light tapping. If the joint is too tight, mark the point where it binds, disassemble the boards, and use a wood chisel to pare away a little more wood at the mark. Dry-fit the joint again and adjust it further, if necessary.

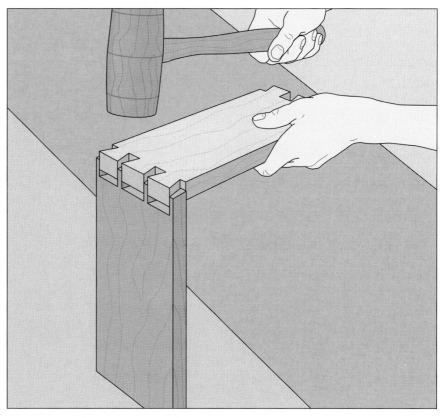

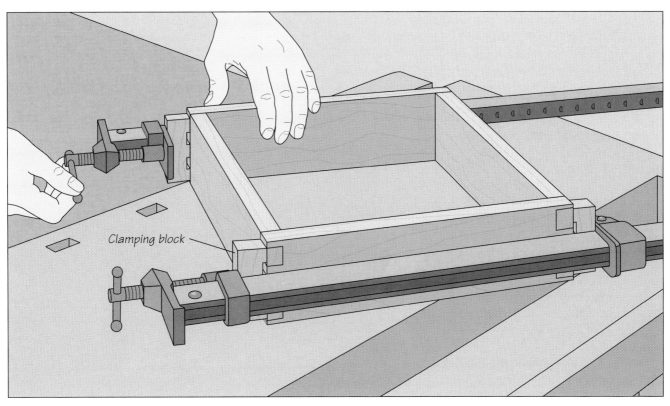

Clamping block

7 Gluing up dovetails

When gluing up a dovetail joint, clamping pressure is applied to the tail boards. To distribute clamping pressure properly, make a specially notched clamping block for each joint. The blocks should be as long as the width of the stock and notched so that they only touch the tails and do not exert pressure on the pins. Spread glue evenly on all the contacting surfaces of the boards, then assemble the joints. Install a bar clamp along each pin board, then tighten the clamps a little at a time *(above)*. Check the carcase for square and adjust the clamping pressure, if necessary.

SHOP TIP

Cutting several tail boards at once
If you are making several dovetail joints, you can streamline the process of cutting the tails by sawing them all at once. Mark the tails on the boards, then stack the pieces together, making sure their edges and ends are aligned. Clamp the stack in a vise, angling the pieces so the right-hand edges of the tails are vertical. Cut the right-hand edges of all the tails, then leave the saw blade in the last kerf as you reposition the stack to cut the left-hand edges. The saw blade will keep the boards in alignment as you shift the stack in the vise.

CUTTING A THROUGH DOVETAIL ON THE TABLE SAW

Cutting the pins

Lay out the pins *(page 118)*, but mark only one end of the board. Then, screw an extension board to the miter gauge that is high enough to support the workpiece during the cuts. Set the angle of the miter gauge to cut the right-hand edges of the pins; use a dovetail square as a guide. To make the cuts, hold the pin board with its inside face against the extension and the marked end on the table, then raise the blade to the shoulder line of the pins. Align the blade with the waste side of the right-hand edge of the center pin, then clamp a stop block on the extension flush against the right-hand edge of the board. Make a cut at the edge of the pin, then clear out about half the waste by cutting a series of kerfs, sliding the piece slightly to the left with each pass. Turn the board end-for-end, butt it against the stop block and the extension and repeat the procedure to make a mirror image of the first cut at the other end *(right, top)*. (Repeat the process for all other identical workpieces.) Then, after turning the board back to the marked end, align the blade with the right-hand edge of the next marked half-pin, reposition the stop block against the edge of the workpiece, and repeat the cutting process on both ends of the board. When the right-hand edges of all the pins are cut and half the waste has been cleared away, reverse the angle of the miter gauge and repeat the procedure to cut the left-hand edges of the pins. This time, continue cutting kerfs into the waste until it is cleared, sliding the board to the right with each pass *(right, bottom)*. To complete the joint, trace the pins on the tail board *(page 121)* and cut the tails by hand *(page 122)* or using a band saw *(page 125)*.

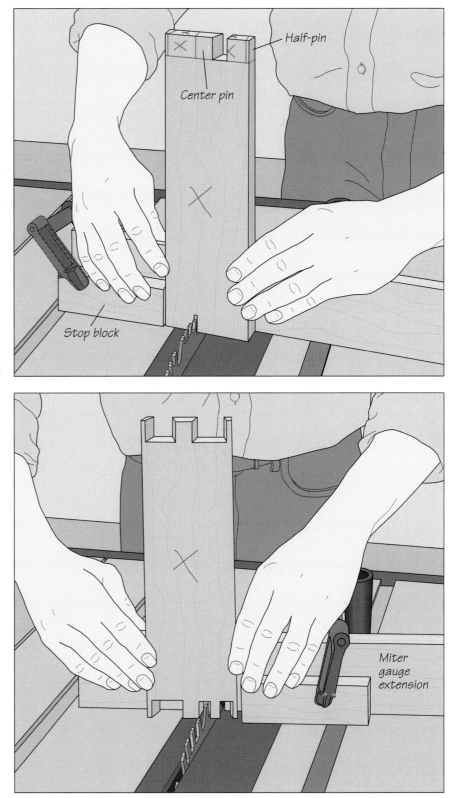

Half-pin

Center pin

Stop block

Miter gauge extension

A THROUGH DOVETAIL JOINT ON THE BAND SAW

1 Cutting the pins

Mark the pins on one end of the work-piece *(page 118)*, then cut them in two stages, first angling the table to the right for one series of cuts, and then to the left for the final ones. Start by tilting the table to match the angle of the dovetail square *(inset)*. Install the rip fence and fasten a wooden L-shaped auxiliary fence to it. Then, set the workpiece outside-face up on the saw table and align the right-hand edge of the first half-pin with the blade. Butt the auxiliary fence against the piece and make the cut, keeping the board flush against the fence. When the blade reaches the shoulder line, stop the cut and turn off the saw. With the blade butted on the shoulder line, hold a stop block against the workpiece and screw it to the auxiliary fence. Turn the piece end-for-end and cut the right-hand edge of the first half-pin at the other end of the board. Turn the workpiece again, align the blade with the marked line for the right-hand edge of the first full pin, butt the auxiliary fence against the workpiece and cut to the stop block *(right)*. Continue turning the work and shifting the rip fence as necessary to cut the right-hand edge of the pins on both ends of the board. Cut the left-hand edge of each pin following the same procedure with the table tilted downward to the left. Finish by using a chisel to remove the waste between the pins *(page 120)*.

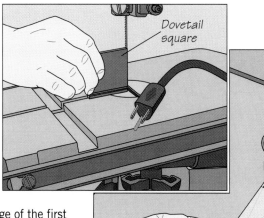

Dovetail square

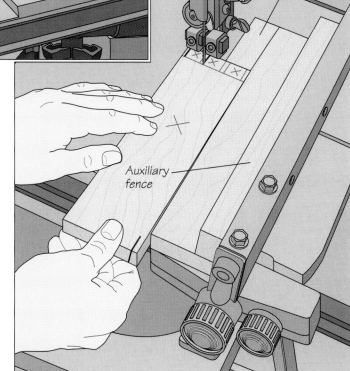

Stop block

Auxiliary fence

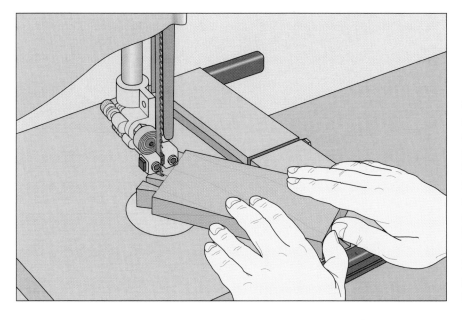

2 Cutting the tails

Use the completed pin board as a guide to outline the tails on the tail board *(page 121)*. To make the cuts and remove the waste, return the table to the horizontal position. Start by sawing out the waste at both edges of the piece with two intersecting cuts. To clear the waste between the tails, nibble at it with the blade, pivoting the piece as necessary to avoid cutting into the tails *(left)*. Test-fit the joint and make any necessary adjustments with a chisel.

CURVED THROUGH DOVETAIL JOINTS

A decorative and challenging variation of the through dovetail joint, the curved through dovetail adds a distinctive touch to any project. The example shown here is a one-sided curved through dovetail, in which only the end of the tail board is curved; the two-sided version requires contours on both the pin and tail boards.

MAKING A CURVED THROUGH DOVETAIL

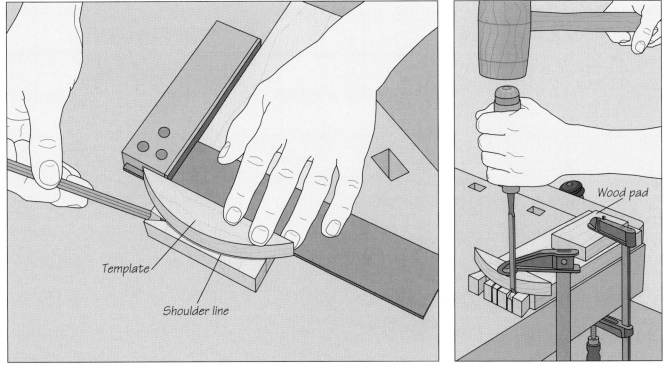

Template

Shoulder line

Wood pad

1 Laying out the tails

It takes three steps to cut a one-sided curved through dovetail. First, cut standard pins in the pin board *(page 118)*; then cut the tails along a curved shoulder line, as shown here; and finally, saw a matching curved rabbet into the bottom of the pins *(step 3)*. To prepare the tail board, set a cutting gauge to the thickness of the pin board and scribe shoulder lines on both edges of the tail board. Make a semicircular template, using as a guide the contour of the dado head you will use in step 3. With the tail board face-down, align the template's curve with the shoulder marks. Using a try square to keep the template perpendicular to the board edges, mark the curved shoulder line on the face of the board *(above, left)*. Use the completed pin board as a guide to outline the tails on the tail board *(page 121)*, extending the marks to the curved shoulder. Cut the tail sides *(page 122)*, then clamp the board face-up on a work surface. Also clamp on the template in line with the shoulder to keep the chisel from straying beyond the waste *(above, right)*. Chisel out the waste between the tails as you would for standard through dovetails *(page 120)*.

2 Preparing to rabbet the pin board

Install the dado head on your table saw and adjust its width to slightly more than the length of the pins. Also install an auxiliary fence and notch it up to the thickness of the pin board *(page 71)*. Next, set the pin board outside-face up on the saw table and center the end of the piece against the outside blade of the dado head, using the miter gauge to keep the board perpendicular to the blade. Adjust the cutting height so the points where the dado head emerges from the table are aligned with the edges of the workpiece. Then mark reference lines on the table insert, using the board edges as a guide *(right)*. Adjust the fence so that the actual cutting width equals the length of the pins, then lower the dado head beneath the table.

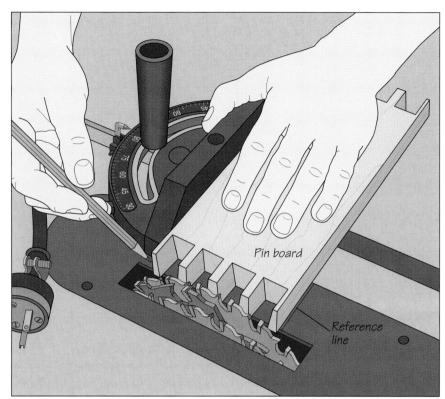

Pin board

Reference line

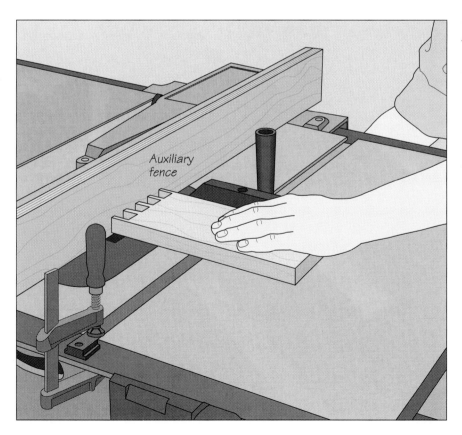

Auxiliary fence

3 Cutting the rabbets

Butt the end of the pin board against the fence and center its edges between the reference lines on the table insert. Slide the miter gauge up against the workpiece, then clamp the gauge in place. Holding the stock firmly in position, turn on the saw and raise the dado head to make a shallow cut in the pins *(left)*. Turn the saw off and test-fit the joint. Make a slightly deeper cut and test again, continuing to cut and test until the joint fits. The process is painstaking, but the results can be well worth your effort.

OUTLINED THROUGH DOVETAIL JOINTS

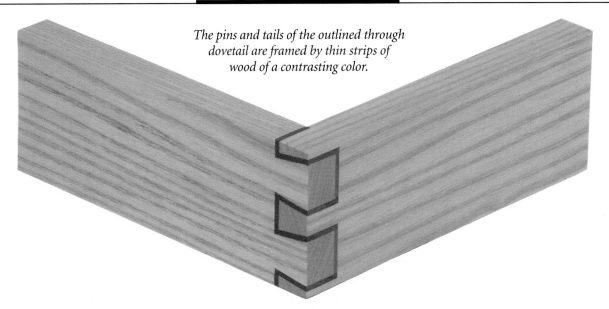

The pins and tails of the outlined through dovetail are framed by thin strips of wood of a contrasting color.

MAKING AN OUTLINED THROUGH DOVETAIL

1 Rabbeting the pin and tail boards
An outlined through dovetail is like the conventional joint, except that space must be created for the contrasting wood—usually a veneer—around and below all pins and tails. The process is fairly simple. Start by cutting rabbets in the inside faces of both mating pieces of the joint. Set a cutting gauge to the stock thickness and scribe a shoulder line around the ends of the boards. Then install a dado head on your table saw and adjust its width so that it is slightly wider than the stock thickness. Also install and notch an auxiliary fence *(page 71)*, and adjust it so that the width of cut equals the stock thickness. Raise the cutting height to the thickness of the veneer. Make a test cut on a scrap board and adjust the cutting height until the veneer fits perfectly in the rabbet. Then cut rabbets at both ends of your stock, feeding each board with the miter gauge *(right)*.

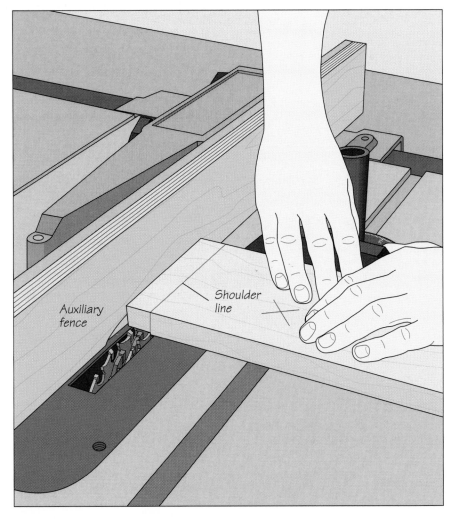

Auxiliary fence

Shoulder line

2 Gluing in the veneer

The joint is outlined in two stages. The veneer strips that fill the rabbets under the pins and tails are glued in before the joint is cut and assembled, as shown at right. The veneer between the pins and tails is inserted after glue-up. For each workpiece, cut two strips of veneer slightly longer and wider than the rabbet cheek, and two clamping blocks with edges the same size as the cheek. Set the workpiece inside-face up on a work surface and spread a thin coating of glue on the cheek. Then clamp the veneer in place, using the clamping block to distribute the pressure evenly *(right)*. Repeat at the other end of the board. Once the glue on all the pieces has cured, cut the pins and tails and glue up the joints.

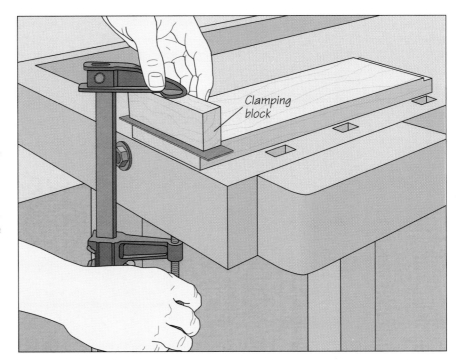

Clamping block

3 Inserting the veneer between the pins and tails

Secure the assembled workpiece in a vise as shown, and use a dovetail saw to cut grooves along the seams between the pins and tails *(left)*. Saw smoothly and evenly, continuing to the shoulder line. Next, cut triangular veneer splines to fit in the grooves. Spread a little glue in the grooves and insert the splines long-edge down *(inset)*. Once the glue has set, cut and sand the splines flush with the boards.

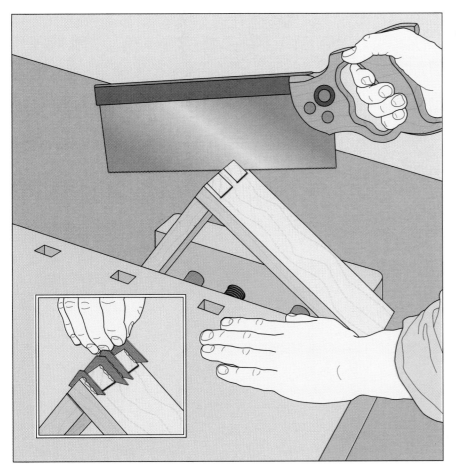

HALF-BLIND DOVETAIL JOINTS

*Half-blind dovetails are often used for drawer fronts.
Virtually as strong as a through dovetail, the half-blind
joint features tails that are visible from the side, but
hidden by the drawer front.*

HAND-CUTTING A HALF-BLIND DOVETAIL

1 Marking the pin board
Mark the outside face of the board
with an X. Then adjust a cutting gauge to
the thickness of the tail board and scribe
a line across the inside face of the pin
board to mark the shoulder line of the pins.
Secure the pin board end-up in a vise and
set the cutting gauge to about one-third
the thickness of the pin board and mark a
line across the end, closer to the outside
than the inside face *(below)*. Next, use a
dovetail square to mark the pins on the
end of the board *(right)*. For the narrow
board shown, follow the spacing pattern
described on page 118. To finish marking,
use a try square and a pencil to extend the
lines on the board end down the inside
face to the shoulder line.

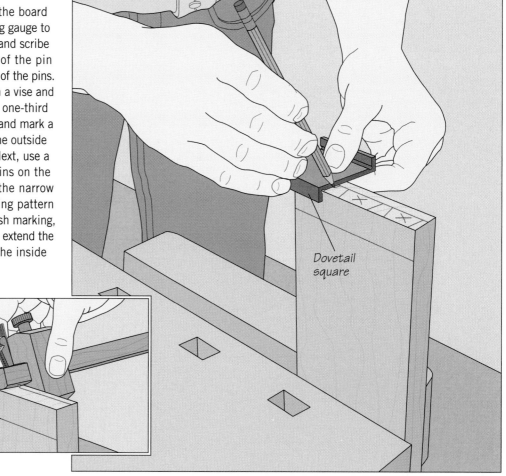

Dovetail
square

Shoulder
line

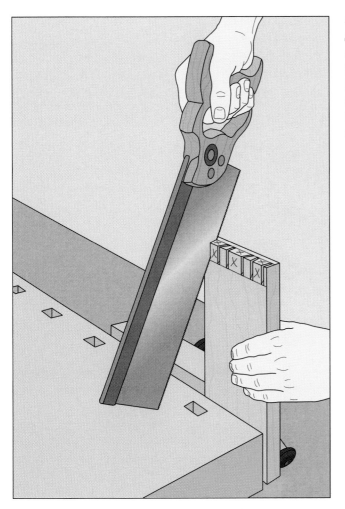

2 Cutting the pins

Secure one pin board in a vise with the outside face of the stock toward you, then cut down along the edges of the pins with a dovetail saw, working from one edge of the board to the other. Hold the board steady and align the saw blade just to the waste side of the cutting lines *(left)*. Use smooth, even strokes, continuing the cuts to the shoulder line and the line on the board end.

3 Removing the waste

Lay the pin board inside-face up on a work surface and clamp a guide block along the waste side of the shoulder line. Use a chisel that is no wider than the narrowest part of the waste area. Starting at one edge of the stock, hold the flat side of the chisel against the guide block. With the chisel perpendicular to the board face, strike the handle with a wooden mallet, making a ⅛-inch-deep cut into the waste. Then hold the chisel bevel-up and square to the board end about ⅛ inch below the top surface and peel away a thin layer of waste. Continue until you reach the scribed line on the board end, then pare away any remaining waste. Repeat the process with the remaining waste sections *(below)*. Finish the joint by marking and cutting the tails as you would for a through dovetail joint *(page 121)*. When marking, remember that the tails of this joint will be shallower than those of a through joint because they extend only to the bottom of the blind pins.

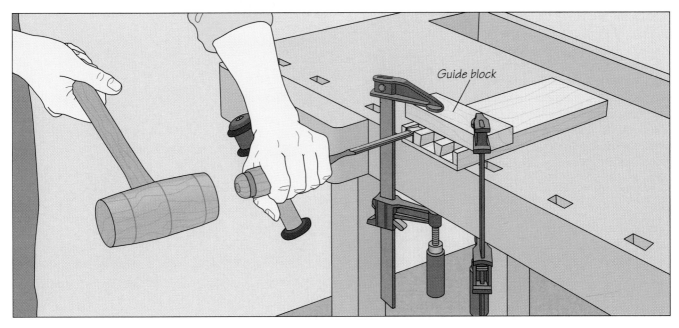

Guide block

BOX JOINTS

Originally developed for mass-produced carcases like packing crates and jewelry boxes, the box joint now lends strength and a traditional look to modern furniture.

CUTTING A BOX JOINT ON THE TABLE SAW

1 Making the jig

The notches for a box joint are cut one after another on the table saw using a dado head and a simple jig made from an extension board clamped to the miter gauge. First adjust the width of the dado head so that the pins and notches on the edges of the pieces will all be the same size. Make the cutting height equal to the stock thickness, clamp the extension onto the miter gauge, and feed it into the dado head to cut a notch. Slide the extension along the miter gauge so the gap between the notch and the dado head is equal to the notch width, then screw the extension to the gauge. Feed the extension into the blades to cut a second notch *(right)*. Then, insert a tight-fitting wooden key in the first notch so it projects at least 1 inch from the extension.

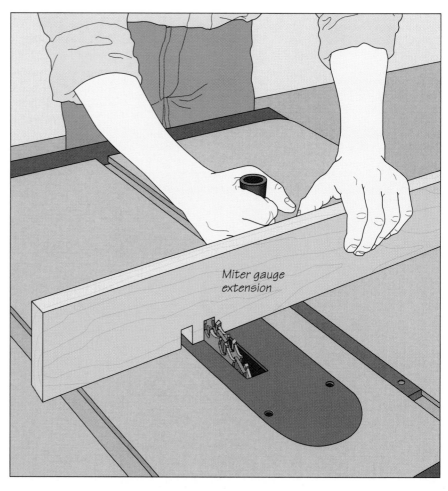

Miter gauge extension

2 Cutting the notches in the first board
Butt the edge of the board against the key and hold its face flat against the extension. Turn on the saw and feed the piece into the dado head, hooking your thumbs around the extension to steady the piece during the cut *(right)*. Then lift the workpiece clear of the dado head and return the miter gauge to the front of the table. Fit the notch you just cut over the key and make the second cut. Continue cutting notches in this manner until you reach the opposite side of the workpiece.

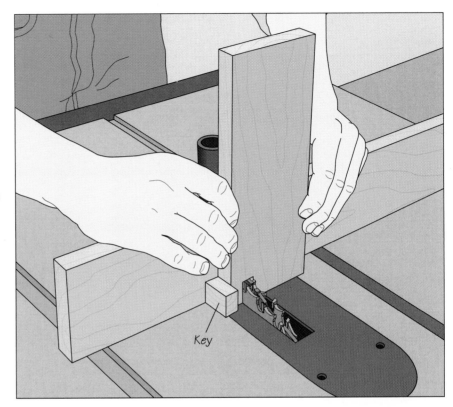

Key

Mating board

3 Cutting the notches in the mating board
Fit the final notch you cut in the first piece over the key, then butt one edge of the mating board against the first board. Holding both boards firmly against the extension, feed the mating piece into the dado head *(left)*. Continue cutting notches in the mating board following the same procedure you used on the first board.

FINGER JOINTS

*An attractive and solid variation of the box joint,
the finger joint derives its strength from the
large gluing area provided by its numerous inter-
woven fingers and notches. It is most often used
to assemble drawers and small carcases.*

A FINGER JOINT ON THE RADIAL ARM SAW

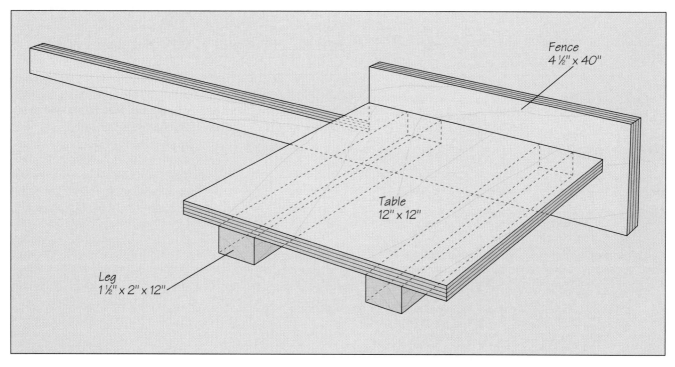

Fence
4 ½" x 40"

Table
12" x 12"

Leg
1 ½" x 2" x 12"

1 Making and setting up the jig

The jig shown above makes cutting accurate finger joints on the radial arm saw an easy task. Cut the table and fence from ¾-inch plywood, and the legs from solid wood. Refer to the illustration for suggested dimensions. Cut a 3-inch-by-25-inch corner section from one end of the fence using a band or saber saw; the cutout will provide clearance for the motor and blade guard when the jig is installed on the radial arm saw. Fasten the legs to the underside of the table with countersunk screws. To assemble the jig, slip the fence into its slot in the saw table, then position the left edge of the jig table against the right edge of the fence's cutout, and screw the two pieces of plywood together.

2 Cutting the first notch

Tilt the saw blade to the horizontal position, then set both workpieces on edge against the jig fence. The depth of the fingers and notches will be the thickness of the stock; set the depth of cut by extending the boards over the edge of the blade by the proper amount. Then slip a shim that is the same thickness as the saw blade under the workpiece that rests against the fence. Clamp the boards to the fence, using protective wood pads and making sure the board ends are aligned. Install a handscrew on the saw arm to stop blade travel as soon as each cut is completed. For the first cut, adjust the blade to the same level as the shim. Then, with the blade guard covering as much of the blade as possible, pull the blade through the cut *(right)*. Return the blade behind the fence and turn off the saw.

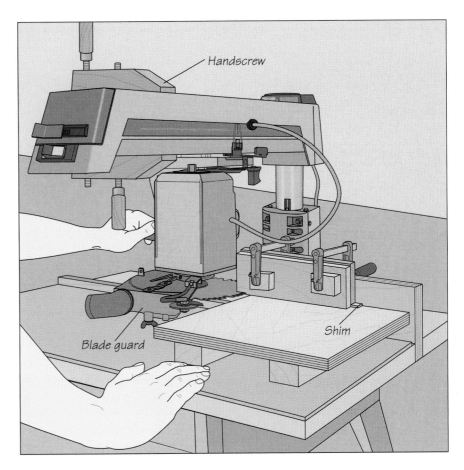

Handscrew

Blade guard

Shim

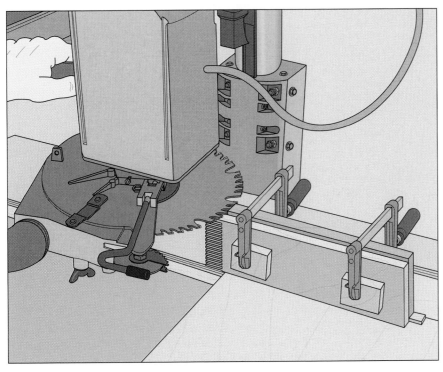

3 Cutting the remaining notches and fingers

For each of the remaining cuts, raise the blade by an amount equal to twice the thickness of the shim. Refer to your saw's manual to calculate the number of turns of the pedestal crank that will accomplish this. Use your left hand to feed the blade, leaving your right hand free to adjust the blade height; be sure to slide the blade behind the fence before raising the cutting height. Continue in this manner until all the notches and fingers have been cut *(left)*.

JAPANESE JOINERY

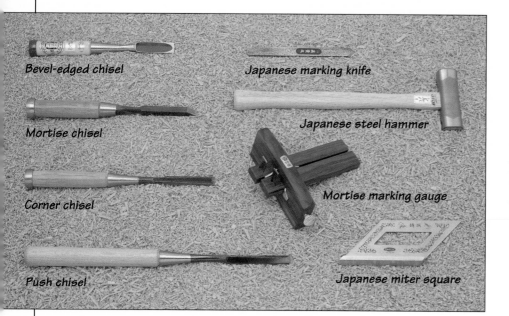

Bevel-edged chisel

Japanese marking knife

Mortise chisel

Japanese steel hammer

Corner chisel

Mortise marking gauge

Push chisel

Japanese miter square

Until the great sailing ships established trade routes between Europe and the Orient in the 1500s, the two areas were largely isolated from each other, and their woodworking traditions developed separately. In the West, the evolution of wood joinery can be traced through the history of furniture styles. The half-blind dovetail joint, for example, was born from a need to strengthen a drawer while hiding the connection. Japanese joinery, on the other hand,

A SELECTION OF JAPANESE WOODWORKING TOOLS

Japanese tools differ from their Western counterparts in both subtle and obvious ways. A Japanese mortise gauge works much like its Western equivalent, except that it is fitted with small blades instead of pins. And, the width of a mortise is set by adjusting the gap between the two beams, rather than by moving the stock in relation to the blades.

Like Western-style chisels, the Japanese versions are designed for specific purposes: The push chisel has a triangular blade for cleaning up dovetail joint pins and tails; the mortise chisel features a thick, square blade with slightly concave sides to reduce friction; and the corner chisel is used to square large mortises. But a Japanese chisel made with a steel-hooped handle is strong enough to withstand being struck by a steel hammer.

Japanese saws and planes depart from Western design altogether because they cut on the pull stroke, rather than the push stroke. The ryoba is a combination saw, with rip teeth on one edge and crosscut teeth on the other. The dozuki, with

slightly set teeth, is used in joinery and fine bench work. The flush-cutting kugi-hiki is used for delicate cleanup work. It has a flexible blade for trimming tenons or dowels without marking the surround-

ing surface because its teeth have no set. The chamfer plane in the photo features screw-adjusted fences; the tool is designed to shape the beveled molding commonly used in Japanese doors.

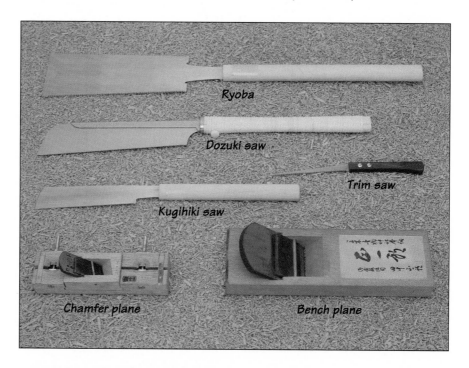

Ryoba

Dozuki saw

Trim saw

Kugihiki saw

Chamfer plane

Bench plane

evolved not from furniture making but from the design and construction of religious shrines and temples. In addition, a Japanese woodworker traditionally wore the hat of architect in addition to that of artisan and carpenter. In fact, the closest English equivalent of *daiku*, the Japanese word often translated as "carpenter," is "master builder."

In Japan, carpentry developed within a family guild system characterized by fierce competition and secrecy. In addition to designing joints that fulfilled the basic requirements of structural strength and esthetic harmony with Eastern philosophical concepts, rival guilds sought to develop increasingly complex joints whose interlocking components were invisible when assembled. Of the 400 joints still in use in Japan today, many are descended from these secret joints.

The complexity of Japanese joinery owes as much to native building materials as to the philosophy behind the craft. In Japan, the stone and clay necessary for brickmaking are scarce, and therefore the mason's art did not develop to the level it did in Europe and China. On the other hand, Japan's rich volcanic soil grows a wide variety of trees. The abundance of species, as well as their woods' structural resistance to earthquakes, fostered the ancient tradition of building from wood—everything from sliding rice paper doors to Shinto temples.

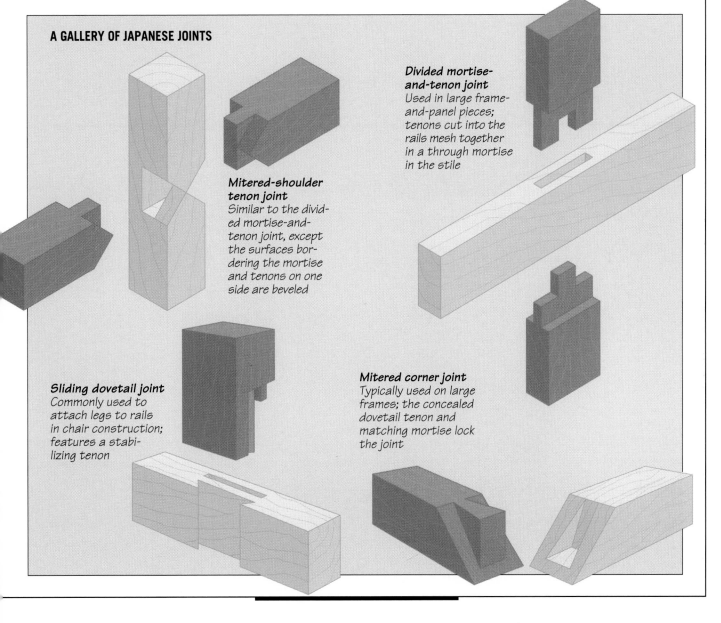

A GALLERY OF JAPANESE JOINTS

Divided mortise-and-tenon joint
Used in large frame-and-panel pieces; tenons cut into the rails mesh together in a through mortise in the stile

Mitered-shoulder tenon joint
Similar to the divided mortise-and-tenon joint, except the surfaces bordering the mortise and tenons on one side are beveled

Sliding dovetail joint
Commonly used to attach legs to rails in chair construction; features a stabilizing tenon

Mitered corner joint
Typically used on large frames; the concealed dovetail tenon and matching mortise lock the joint

Unlike inorganic building materials like brick and stone, wood retains a warmth that serves as a reminder that it was once a living thing. In Japan, craftsmen hold the view that wood has a soul, inspiring a sense of reverence that still surrounds traditional methods of joinery in Japan.

For Japanese woodworkers, their art begins with respect for the tools. Despite advances in technology that have given the modern woodworker portable power tools and stationary machines, many Japanese woodworkers still rely mainly on hand tools that have remained virtually unchanged for centuries *(page 136)*. For example, a traditional Japanese plane, or *kanna*, is a simple affair, having a hardwood body, a thick blade, and a cap iron. Japanese planes cut on the pull stroke, and their blades are laminated with a thin layer of high-carbon steel forming the cutting edge, backed by a thick strip of soft, low-carbon steel to absorb shock when planing knotty grain. The blades of Japanese chisels, or *nomi*, are laminated like plane blades, with a hard, hollow-ground back supported by a thick, shock-absorbing top of soft steel. A Japanese saw, or *nokogiri*, also cuts on the pull stroke, so its blade can be much thinner than the Western counterpart and its teeth can be finely set.

Only care, diligent maintenance, and respect for these tools can produce

Pinned carcase joint
A corner joint used in carcases constructed with heavy panels; the stopped tongue provides alignment while the through tenons resist shear stress

Interlocking-tenon joint
Featured in chair and staircase construction, this locking joint attaches two or more pieces

Shelf support joint
Used for shelves that must bear heavy loads; end of shelf sits in stopped dado while blind tenon holds the shelf straight and tightens joint

the elaborate and precise joints seen on these pages.

Japanese joints are grouped into two main categories. A splicing joint, or *tsugi*, joins two pieces end-to-end to create a longer one. A *shiguchi*, connects two or more pieces at an angle. Because many Japanese houses have few pieces of furniture, the traditional Japanese joints originated as carpentry joints used in the construction of houses. The *shiguchi* joints shown on the following pages are those that can be applied to cabinetmaking.

In Japan, beauty is an essential element of the art of wood joinery, and the ultimate value of a joint is measured by the subtle combination of its appearance and the builder's skill and speed. A Japanese woodworker aims for perfection with the first saw or chisel cut. Sanding a workpiece to fit is not part of the joinery process. Tradition also requires that any mistake made by a Japanese craftsman remain on the piece to remind him of his humble nature, so every stroke of the saw or plane is crucial, requiring great concentration.

This concentration is demanded by the tools themselves. Although they look deceptively simple to use, Japanese tools require considerable patience and practice to master. As the ancient craftsmen who forged them understood, the key to success is to learn to use the tool with skill and respect.

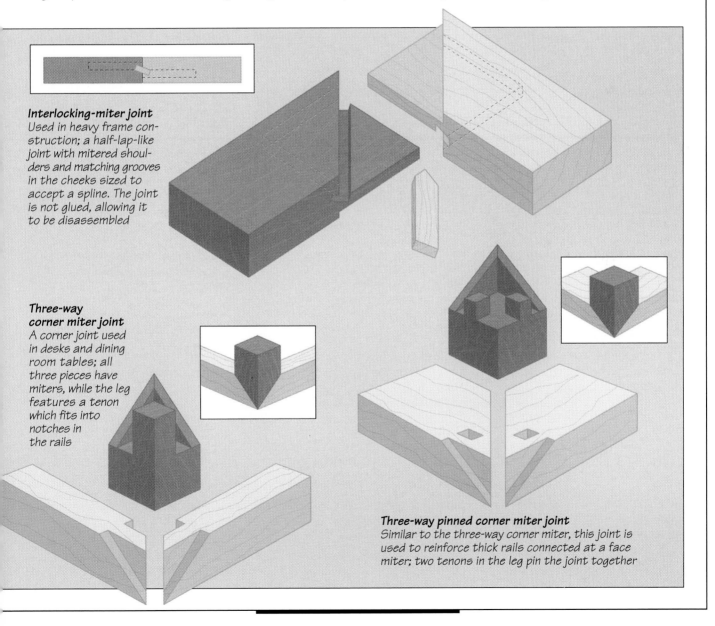

Interlocking-miter joint
Used in heavy frame construction; a half-lap-like joint with mitered shoulders and matching grooves in the cheeks sized to accept a spline. The joint is not glued, allowing it to be disassembled

Three-way corner miter joint
A corner joint used in desks and dining room tables; all three pieces have miters, while the leg features a tenon which fits into notches in the rails

Three-way pinned corner miter joint
Similar to the three-way corner miter, this joint is used to reinforce thick rails connected at a face miter; two tenons in the leg pin the joint together

GLOSSARY

A-B-C

Bench dog: A round or square peg made of metal or wood that fits into a hole in a workbench to hold a workpiece in place.

Bevel cut: A cut made at an angle from face to face along the length or width of a workpiece.

Biscuit: A thin oval wafer of compressed wood, usually beech, that fits into a semicircular slot cut by a plate joiner.

Blind joint: A joint in which the interlocking members are hidden, as in a blind mortise-and-tenon joint. Also known as a stopped cut.

Box joint: A corner joint featuring interlocking fingers.

Butt joinery: A method of joining wood in which the end or edge of one board is set squarely against the face or edge of another; often reinforced when end grain is involved.

Butterfly key joint: An edge-to-edge butt joint reinforced by a wing-shaped key that is often made of a contrasting hardwood for decorative effect.

Carcase: The box-like basic structure of a piece of furniture, formed of solid panels.

Cheek: In a mortise-and-tenon joint, that part of the tenon perpendicular to the shoulder.

Compression: Force that presses the elements of a joint together.

Countersink: Drilling a hole that allows a screw head to lie flush with or slightly below the surface of a workpiece.

Crosscut: A saw cut made across the grain of a workpiece.

D-E-F

Dado: A rectangular channel cut into a workpiece.

Dado head: A blade—or combination of blades and cutters—used to shape dadoes.

Dovetail joint: A corner joined by interlocking pins and tails; the name derives from the shape of the parts.

Dowel: A wood pin used to reinforce certain types of joints.

Edges: The narrower surfaces of a workpiece.

Face jointing: Using a jointer to shave the face of a workpiece until it is flat and square.

Faces: The wider surfaces of a piece of wood.

Featherboard: A board with thin fingers or "feathers" along one end; clamped to the fence or table of a power tool, it holds the workpiece in position.

Fence: An adjustable guide designed to maintain the distance between one edge or face of a workpiece and the cutting edge of a tool.

Finger joint: Similar to a box joint but with narrower meshing fingers, typically less than ⅛ inch wide.

G-H-I-J

Grain: The arrangement and direction of the fibers that make up wood.

Half-lap joint: A lap joint in which the dadoes are half the thickness of the stock; see *lap joint*.

Hanger bolt: A bolt used to hold movable parts of a fixture; one end has screw threads to anchor it in the wood, while the other end features machine threads.

Haunch: An extension of one edge of a tenon intended to increase a mortise-and-tenon joint's resistance to twisting; the haunch can also be used to fill a panel groove, eliminating the need for stopped grooves.

K-L-M-N

Kerf: The cut made by a saw blade.

Lap joint: A joint in which one or both of the mating boards are dadoed to increase gluing area and allow the surfaces of the pieces to lie flush with one another when the joint is assembled.

Miter cut: A cut made obliquely across the face of a workpiece; see *bevel cut*.

Miter joint: A joint in which the mating surfaces meet at an angle other than 90°.

Mortise: A rectangular, round or oval hole.

Mortise-and-tenon joint: A joinery technique in which the projecting tenon of one board fits snugly into the mortise of another.

O-P-Q

Pins: The tapered protrusions cut into the end of one board so that they lock between the tails of the mating piece.

Plain-sawn lumber: Lumber that has been sawn so that the wide surfaces are tangential to the growth rings. Also known as flat-sawn lumber when referring to softwood; see *quartersawn lumber.*

Pocket hole: An angled clearance hole that allows a screw head to be recessed below the surface; often used when joining rails to a tabletop.

Push block or stick: A device used to feed a workpiece into the blade, cutterhead, or bit of a tool to protect the operator's fingers.

Quartersawn lumber: Lumber that has been sawn so the wide surfaces intersect the growth rings at angles between 45° and 90°. Also known as vertical-grained lumber when referring to softwood; see *plain-sawn lumber.*

R-S

Rabbet: A step-like cut made in the edge or end of a board; usually forms part of a joint.

Racking: The twisting of members of a joint in relation to each other; common in frame joints.

Radial section: A viewing plane across the grain perpendicular to the growth rings.

Rail: The board joining legs of a table to which the tabletop is attached; also, the horizontal member of a frame-and-panel assembly.

Rip cut: A cut that follows the grain of a workpiece.

Shear: Stress that causes two halves of a joint to slide against each other.

Shoulder: In a mortise-and-tenon joint, the part of the tenon perpendicular to the cheek. In a dovetail joint, the gaps between pins and tails.

Spline: A thin piece of wood that fits in grooves cut in mating workpieces, reinforcing the joint.

Starved joint: A joint lacking sufficient adhesive; often caused when glue is squeezed out by overtightened clamps.

T-U-V-W-X-Y-Z

Tails: In a dovetail joint, the flaring protrusions cut into the end of one board that mesh with pins in the mating piece.

Tangential: A viewing plane in wood cut along the grain tangent to the growth rings; plain-sawn lumber is sawn tangentially.

Tearout: The ragged edges produced when a blade or cutter tears the wood fibers, rather than cutting them cleanly.

Template: A pattern used with a power tool to produce multiple copies.

Tenon: The blade-like protrusion cut to fit into a mortise.

Tension: Stress that pulls a joint apart at the glue line.

Through bolt: A threaded rod used to reinforce face-glued boards; usually used in making a workbench top or butcher block.

Through joint: A joint in which the end of one piece passes all the way through its mate, as in a through mortise-and-tenon joint.

Tongue-and-groove joint: A joint in which a tongue cut in the edge or end of one piece fits into a groove in the mating piece.

INDEX

ACKNOWLEDGMENTS

The editors wish to thank the following:

JOINERY BASICS
Adjustable Clamp Co., Chicago, IL; Steiner-Lamello A.G. Switzerland/Colonial Saw Co. Kingston, MA

BUTT JOINTS
Adjustable Clamp Co., Chicago, IL; American Tool Cos., Inc., Lincoln, NE; Delta International Machinery/Porter Cable, Guelph, Ont.; Hitachi Power Tools U.S.A. Ltd., Norcross, GA; Robert Larson Company, Inc., San Francisco, CA; Lee Valley Tools Ltd., Ottawa, Ont.; Shopsmith, Inc., Montreal, Que.; Steiner-Lamello A.G. Switzerland/Colonial Saw Co. Kingston, MA; Veritas Tools Inc., Ottawa, Ont./Ogdensburg, NY; Vermont American Corp., Lincolnton, NC and Louisville, KY; M.E. Wyant Distributing Inc., Nottawa, Ont.

MITER JOINTS
Adjustable Clamp Co., Chicago, IL; Black & Decker/Elu Power Tools, Towson, MD; Delta International Machinery/Porter Cable, Guelph, Ont.; Hempe Manufacturing Co., Inc., New Berlin, WI; Sandvik Saws and Tools Co., Scranton, PA; Sears, Roebuck and Co., Chicago, IL; Steiner-Lamello A.G. Switzerland/Colonial Saw Co. Kingston, MA; Vermont American Corp., Lincolnton, NC and Louisville, KY

LAP, RABBET, GROOVE, AND DADO JOINTS
Adjustable Clamp Co., Chicago, IL; American Tool Cos., Inc., Lincoln, NE; Black & Decker/Elu Power Tools, Towson, MD; Delta International Machinery/Porter Cable, Guelph, Ont.; Freud Westmore Tools, Ltd., Mississauga, Ont.; Great Neck Saw Mfrs. Inc. (Buck Bros. Division), Millbury, MA; Griset Industries, Inc., Santa Ana, CA; Hempe Manufacturing Co., Inc., New Berlin, WI; Sandvik Saws and Tools Co., Scranton, PA; Sears, Roebuck and Co., Chicago, IL; Shopsmith, Inc., Montreal, Que.

MORTISE-AND-TENON JOINTS
Adjustable Clamp Co., Chicago, IL; American Tool Cos., Inc., Lincoln, NE; Black & Decker/Elu Power Tools, Towson, MD; Delta International Machinery/Porter Cable, Guelph, Ont.; Freud Westmore Tools, Ltd., Mississauga, Ont.; General Tools Manufacturing Co., Inc., New York, NY; Great Neck Saw Mfrs. Inc. (Buck Bros. Division), Millbury, MA; Frank Klausz, Frank's Cabinet Shop, Inc., Pluckemin, NJ; Robert Larson Company, Inc., San Francisco, CA; Leichtung Workshops, Cleveland, OH; Leigh Industries Ltd., Port Coquitlam, B.C.; Sandvik Saws and Tools Co., Scranton, PA

DOVETAIL AND BOX JOINTS
Adjustable Clamp Co., Chicago, IL; American Tool Cos., Inc., Lincoln, NE; Black & Decker/Elu Power Tools, Towson, MD; Delta International Machinery/Porter Cable, Guelph, Ont.; Freud Westmore Tools, Ltd., Mississauga, Ont.; Great Neck Saw Mfrs. Inc. (Buck Bros. Division), Millbury, MA; Robert Larson Company, Inc., San Francisco, CA; Leichtung Workshops, Cleveland, OH; Leigh Industries Ltd., Port Coquitlam, B.C.; Sandvik Saws and Tools Co., Scranton, PA; Sears, Roebuck and Co., Chicago, IL

JAPANESE JOINERY
Garrett Wade Company, Inc., New York, NY; Henry Lanz, New York, NY; Toshio Odate, Woodbury, CT

The following persons also assisted in the preparation of this book:

Lorraine Doré, Graphor Consultation, Geneviève Monette

PICTURE CREDITS

Cover Robert Chartier
6, 7 Bill Truslow
8, 9 Doug McKay
10, 11 Chris Wimpey
43 Courtesy Stanley Tools, Division of the Stanley Works
87 Courtesy Delta International Machinery/Porter Cable